LET US BECOME
FRIENDS OF JESUS

MEDITATIONS ON PRAYER

LET US BECOME FRIENDS OF JESUS

MEDITATIONS ON PRAYER

POPE BENEDICT XVI

Compiled by Jeanne Kun

the**WORD** among us® *press*

Published by The Word Among Us Press
7115 Guilford Road
Frederick, Maryland 21704
www.wau.org

17 16 15 14 13   1 2 3 4 5

ISBN: 978-1-59325-224-3
eISBN: 978-1-59325-446-9

Pope Benedict XVI's homilies and addresses are taken from the Vatican translation and can be found on the Vatican website, www.vatican.va. Used with permission of Libreria Editrice Vaticana.

Unless otherwise noted, Scripture texts used in this work are from The Catholic Edition of the Revised Standard Version of the Bible, copyright 1965, 1966 by the Division of Christian Education of the National Council of the Churches of Christ in the United States of America. Used by permission. All rights reserved.

Scripture texts marked "NAB" are taken from the New American Bible, revised edition © 2010, 1991, 1986, 1970 Confraternity of Christian Doctrine, Washington, D.C. Used by permission. All rights reserved.

Cover design by John Hamilton Design
Cover photo © Alessandra Benedetti/Corbis

Made and printed in the United States of America

Library of Congress Cataloging-in-Publication Data

Benedict XVI, Pope, 1927-
  Let us become friends of Jesus : meditations on prayer / Pope Benedict XVI ; compiled by Jeanne Kun.
    pages cm
  ISBN 978-1-59325-224-3
  1. Prayer--Catholic Church--Meditations. I. Kun, Jeanne, 1951- II. Title.
  BV210.3.B46 2013
  248.3'2--dc23
                                    2012045428

CONTENTS

VII. Mary, Pray for Us! / 129

EDITOR'S PREFACE

Let us become friends of Jesus, let us try to know him
all the more! Let us live in dialogue with him! Let us
learn from him how to live aright, let us be his witnesses!
Then we become people who love and then
we act aright. Then we are truly alive.
—Pope Benedict XVI, Homily, Holy Thursday, April 1, 2010

The deepest desire of the human heart is to be united to God. It is in prayer that we speak to God and seek to touch his heart, and in turn, God speaks to us, listens to us, and opens his heart to us. So it is in prayer that our longing for union with God begins to be satisfied. And as we begin to pray regularly, we are rewarded: we enter into a true friendship with Jesus, who reveals to us the face of God.

During the eight years of his pontificate, Pope Benedict continually stressed that faith requires a personal encounter with Christ, and such a personal encounter happens in prayer. He continually recounted the innumerable blessings that come from prayer, even while acknowledging that it requires effort: "The experience of prayer is a challenge to everyone, a 'grace' to invoke, a gift of the One to whom we turn" (General Audience, St. Peter's Square, May 11, 2011). Rich in personal experience and in wisdom, this holy man is well qualified to inspire and guide us in the ways of prayer. With the insight and warmth of a gifted pastor, he encourages us to pause often and long before

God. He also shows us how we can approach God—whether through Scripture, the Eucharist, or meditation, or simply by gazing on a crucifix.

The meditations on prayer brought together in this collection have been selected from Pope Benedict's audiences, homilies, addresses, and writings from the eight years of his pontificate. These selections, while grouped in major themes about which he frequently spoke and taught, have all been chosen for the purpose of drawing us into a deeper experience of prayer and thus into a deeper relationship and union with God. Among the selections are several meditations from Pope Benedict's catechesis on prayer, which he presented at his weekly Wednesday audiences.

The Word Among Us Press is delighted to bring you this book. It is our hope that through your own prayerful reflection on Pope Benedict's meditations, this invitation of his will be fulfilled in you: that you become a true and devoted friend of Jesus!

Jeanne Kun

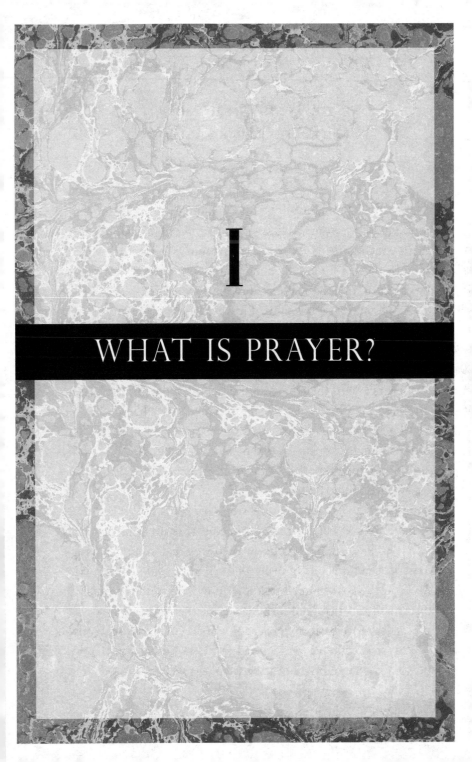

I

WHAT IS PRAYER?

Prayer Expresses
Our Desire for God

Man bears within him a thirst for the infinite, a longing for eternity, a quest for beauty, a desire for love, a need for light and for truth which impel him toward the Absolute; man bears within him the desire for God. And man knows, in a certain way, that he can turn to God; he knows he can pray to him.

St. Thomas Aquinas, one of the greatest theologians of history, defines prayer as "an expression of man's desire for God." This attraction to God, which God himself has placed in man, is the soul of prayer that then takes on a great many forms in accordance with the history, the time, the moment, the grace, and even the sin of every person praying. Man's history has in fact known various forms of prayer because he has developed different kinds of openness to the "Other" and to the "Beyond," so that we may recognize prayer as an experience present in every religion and culture.

Indeed, dear brothers and sisters, prayer is not linked to a specific context but is written on the heart of every person and of every civilization. Of course, when we speak of prayer as an experience of the human being as such, of the *homo orans*, it is necessary to bear in mind that it is an inner attitude before it is a series of practices and formulas, a manner of being in God's presence before performing acts of worship or speaking words.

Prayer is centered and rooted in the inmost depths of the person; it is therefore not easily decipherable and, for the same reason, can be subject to misunderstanding and mystification. In this sense too, we can understand the expression: prayer is difficult. In fact, prayer is the place par excellence of free giving, of striving for the Invisible, the Unexpected, and the Ineffable. Therefore, the experience of prayer is a challenge to everyone, a grace to invoke, a gift of the One to whom we turn.

In prayer, in every period of history, man considers himself and his situation before God, from God, and in relation to God, and he experiences being a creature in need of help, incapable of obtaining on his own the fulfillment of his life and his hope. The philosopher Ludwig Wittgenstein mentioned that "prayer means feeling that the world's meaning is outside the world."

In the dynamic of this relationship with the One who gives meaning to existence, with God, prayer has one of its typical expressions in the gesture of kneeling. It is a gesture that has in itself a radical ambivalence. In fact, I can be forced to kneel—a condition of indigence and slavery—but I can also kneel spontaneously, declaring my limitations and therefore my being in need of Another. To him I declare I am weak, needy, "a sinner."

In the experience of prayer, the human creature expresses all his self-awareness, all that he succeeds in grasping of his own existence, and, at the same time, he turns with his whole being to the One before whom he stands, directs his soul to that Mystery from which he expects the fulfillment of his deepest desires and help to overcome the neediness of his own life. In this turning to "Another," in directing himself "beyond," lies the essence of prayer, as an experience of a reality that overcomes the tangible and the contingent.

Yet only in God who reveals himself does man's seeking find complete fulfillment. The prayer that is openness and elevation of the heart to God thus becomes a personal relationship with him. And even if man forgets his Creator, the living, true God does not cease to call man first to the mysterious encounter of prayer.

As the *Catechism* says:

> In prayer, the faithful God's initiative of love always comes first; our own first step is always a response. As God gradually reveals himself and reveals man to himself, prayer appears as a reciprocal call, a covenant drama. Through words and actions, this drama engages the heart. It unfolds throughout the whole history of salvation. (2567)

Dear brothers and sisters, let us learn to pause longer before God, who revealed himself in Jesus Christ. Let us learn to recognize in silence, in our own hearts, his voice that calls us and leads us back to the depths of our existence, to the source of life, to the source of salvation, to enable us to go beyond the limitations of our life, and to open ourselves to God's dimension, to the relationship with him, who is infinite Love.

—General Audience, St. Peter's Square, May 11, 2011

WHY DO WE NEED TO PRAY?

Prayer is not only the breath of the soul, but, to make use of a metaphor, it is also the oasis of peace from which we can draw the water that nourishes our spiritual life and transforms our existence. God draws us toward him, offering us enlightenment and consolation, and enabling us to scale the mountain of holiness so that we may be ever closer to him. . . .

Contemplating the Lord is at the same time both fascinating and awe inspiring. Fascinating, because he draws us to him and enraptures our hearts by uplifting them, carrying them to his heights where we experience the peace and beauty of his love; awe inspiring, because he lays bare our human weakness, our inadequacy, the effort to triumph over the evil one who endangers our life, that thorn embedded also in our flesh. In prayer, in the daily contemplation of the Lord, we receive the strength of God's love and feel that St. Paul's words to the Christians of Rome are true . . . :

> For I am sure that neither death, nor life, nor angels, nor principalities, nor things present, nor things to come, nor powers, nor height, nor depth, nor anything else in all creation, will be able to separate us from the love of God in Christ Jesus our Lord. (Romans 8:38-39)

In a world in which we risk relying solely on the efficiency and power of human means, we are called to rediscover and to witness to the power of God that is communicated in prayer, with which every day we grow in conforming our life to that of Christ. As Paul says, Christ "was crucified in weakness, but lives by the power of God. For we are weak in him, but in dealing with you we shall live with him by the power of God" (2 Corinthians 13:4).

Dear friends, in the past century, Albert Schweitzer, a Protestant theologian who won the Nobel Peace Prize, said, "Paul is a mystic and nothing but a mystic," that is, a man truly in love with Christ and so united to him that he could say, "Christ lives in me" (cf. Galatians 2:20). The mysticism of St. Paul is founded not only on the exceptional events he lived through, but also on his daily and intense relationship with the Lord who always sustained him with his grace. Mysticism did not distance him from reality; on the contrary, it gave him the strength to live each day for Christ and to build the Church to the ends of the world of that time. Union with God does not distance us from the world but gives us the strength to remain really in the world, to do what must be done in the world.

Thus, in our life of prayer as well, we can perhaps have moments of special intensity in which we feel the Lord's presence is more vivid, especially in situations of aridity, of difficulty, of suffering, of an apparent absence of God. Only if we are grasped by Christ's love will we be equal to facing every adversity, convinced, like Paul, that we can do all things in the One who gives us strength (cf. Philippians 4:13). Therefore, the more room we make for prayer, the more we will see our life transformed and enlivened by the tangible power of God's love.

This is what happened, for example, to Blessed Mother Teresa of Calcutta, who found in contemplation of Jesus and even in long periods of aridity the ultimate reason and incredible strength to recognize him in the poor and abandoned, in spite of her fragility. Contemplation of Christ in our life does not alienate us—as I have already said—from reality. Rather, it enables us to share even more in human events, because the Lord, in attracting us to him through prayer, enables us to make ourselves present and close to every brother and sister in his love.

—General Audience, Paul VI Audience Hall, June 13, 2012

The Spirit Prays in Us

Paul teaches us an important thing: he says that there is no true prayer without the presence of the Spirit within us. He wrote,

> The Spirit helps us in our weakness; for we do not know how to pray as we ought, but the Spirit himself intercedes for us with sighs too deep for words. And he who searches the hearts of men knows what is the mind of the Spirit, because the Spirit intercedes for the saints according to the will of God. (Romans 8:26-27)

It is as if to say that the Holy Spirit, that is, the Spirit of the Father and of the Son, is henceforth, as it were, the soul of our soul, the most secret part of our being, from which an impulse of prayer rises ceaselessly to God, whose words we cannot even begin to explain.

In fact, the Spirit, ever alert within us, completes what is lacking in us and offers to the Father our worship as well as our deepest aspirations.

This, of course, requires a degree of great and vital communion with the Spirit. It is an invitation to be increasingly sensitive, more attentive to this presence of the Spirit in us, to transform it into prayer, to feel this presence and thus to learn to pray, to speak to the Father as children in the Holy Spirit.

—General Audience, St. Peter's Square, November 15, 2006

GOD INITIATES OUR PRAYER

God, in being Father, has two dimensions. First of all, God is our Father because he is our Creator. Each one of us, each man and each woman, is a miracle of God, is wanted by him, and is personally known by him. When it says in the Book of Genesis that the human being is created in the image of God (cf. 1:27), it tries to express this precise reality: God is our Father; for him we are not anonymous, impersonal beings but have a name. And a phrase in the psalms always moves me when I pray: "Your hands have made and fashioned me," says the psalmist (119:73). In this beautiful image, each one of us can express his personal relationship with God. "Your hands have fashioned me. You thought of me and created and wanted me."

Nonetheless, this is still not enough. The Spirit of Christ opens us to a second dimension of God's fatherhood, beyond creation, since Jesus is the "Son" in the full sense of "consubstantial with the Father," as we profess in the creed. Becoming a human being like us, with his Incarnation, death, and resurrection, Jesus in his turn accepts us into his humanity and even into his being Son so that we, too, may enter into his specific belonging to God. Of course, our being children of God does not have the fullness of Jesus' sonship. We must increasingly become so throughout the journey of our Christian existence, developing in the following of Christ and in communion with him so as to enter ever more intimately into the relationship of love with God the Father that sustains our life.

It is this fundamental reality that is disclosed to us when we open ourselves to the Holy Spirit and he makes us turn to God, saying, "Abba! Father!" We have truly preceded creation, entering into adoption with Jesus; united, we are really in God and are his children in a new way, in a new dimension.

In the Letter to the Galatians, in fact, the apostle says that the Spirit cries, "Abba! Father!" in us (4:6). In the Letter to the Romans, he says that it is we who cry, "Abba! Father!" (8:15). And St. Paul wants to make us understand that Christian prayer is never one way; it never happens in only one direction from us to God; it is never merely "an action of ours" but rather is the expression of a reciprocal relationship in which God is the first to act. It is the Holy Spirit who cries in us, and we are able to cry because the impetus comes from the Holy Spirit.

We would not be able to pray were the desire for God, for being children of God, not engraved in the depths of our heart. Since he came into existence, *homo sapiens* has always been in search of God and endeavors to speak with God because God has engraved himself in our hearts. The first initiative, therefore, comes from God, and with baptism, once again God acts in us, the Holy Spirit acts in us; he is the prime initiator of prayer so that we may really converse with God and say, "Abba" to God. Hence, his presence opens our prayers and our lives; it opens onto the horizons of the Trinity and of the Church.

—General Audience, St. Peter's Square, May 23, 2012

We Pray with the Entire Church

We realize . . . that the prayer of the Spirit of Christ in us and ours in him is not solely an individual act but an act of the entire Church. In praying, our heart is opened; not only do we enter into communion with God but actually with all the children of God, because we are one body. When we address the Father in our inner room in silence and in recollection, we are never alone. Those who speak to God are not alone. We are within the great prayer of the Church; we are part of a great symphony that the Christian community in all the parts of the earth and in all epochs raises to God. Naturally, the musicians and instruments differ—and this is an element of enrichment—but the melody of praise is one and in harmony. Every time, then, that we shout or say, "Abba! Father!" it is the Church, the whole communion of people in prayer, that supports our invocation, and our invocation is an invocation of the Church.

This is also reflected in the wealth of charisms and ministries and tasks that we carry out in the community. St. Paul writes to the Christians of Corinth, "There are varieties of gifts, but the same Spirit; and there are varieties of service, but the same Lord; and there are varieties of working, but it is the same God who inspires them all in every one" (1 Corinthians 12:4-6).

Prayer guided by the Holy Spirit, who makes us say, "Abba! Father!" with Christ and in Christ, inserts us into the great mosaic of the family of God in which each one has a place and an important role, in profound unity with the whole. . . .

Dear brothers and sisters, let us learn to savor in our prayers the beauty of being friends, indeed children of God, of being able to call on him with the trust that a child has for the parents who love him. Let us open our prayers to the action of the Holy Spirit so that he may cry to God in us, "Abba! Father!" and so that our prayers may transform and constantly convert our way of thinking and our action to bring us ever more closely into line with Jesus Christ, the only begotten Son of God.

—General Audience, St. Peter's Square, May 23, 2012

To Pray Is to Have Hope

Those who pray never lose hope, even when they find themselves in a difficult and even humanly hopeless plight. Sacred Scripture teaches us this, and Church history bears witness to this. In fact, how many examples we could cite of situations in which it was precisely prayer that sustained the journey of saints and of the Christian people!

Among the testimonies of our epoch, I would like to mention the examples of two saints: Teresa Benedicta of the Cross, Edith Stein, whose feast is celebrated on August 9, and Maximilian Mary Kolbe, whose feast is commemorated on August 14, the eve of the Solemnity of the Assumption of the Blessed Virgin Mary. Both ended their earthly lives with martyrdom in the concentration camp of Auschwitz. Their lives might seem to have been a defeat, but it is precisely in their martyrdom that the brightness of love, which dispels the gloom of selfishness and hatred, shines forth. The following words are attributed to St. Maximilian Kolbe, who is said to have spoken them when the Nazi persecution was raging: "Hatred is not a creative force; only love is creative." And heroic proof of his love was the generous offering he made of himself in exchange for a fellow prisoner, an offer that culminated in his death in the starvation bunker on August 14, 1941.

On August 6 of the following year, three days before her tragic end, Edith Stein approached some sisters in the monastery of Echt, in the Netherlands, and said to them, "I am ready for anything. Jesus is also here in our midst. Thus far I have been able to pray very well, and I have said with all my heart: '*Ave, Crux, spes unica*' ['Hail, O Cross, our only hope']." Witnesses who managed to escape the terrible massacre recounted that while Teresa Benedicta of the Cross, dressed in the Carmelite habit, was making her way—consciously—toward death, she distinguished herself by her peaceful conduct, her serene attitude, and her calm behavior, attentive to the needs of all. Prayer was the secret of this saint, co-patroness of Europe, who "even after she found the truth in the peace of the contemplative life, . . . was to live to the full the mystery of the Cross" (Apostolic Letter *Spes Aedificandi,* 8).

"Hail Mary!" was the last prayer on the lips of St. Maximilian Mary Kolbe as he offered his arm to the person who was about to kill him with an injection of phenolic acid. It is moving to note how humble and trusting recourse to Our Lady is always a source of courage and serenity. . . . Let us renew our trust in her who from heaven watches over us with motherly love at every moment. In fact, we say this in the familiar prayer of the Hail Mary, asking her to pray for us "now and at the hour of our death."

—General Audience, Castel Gandolfo, August 13, 2008

We Are Children of the Father

When Jesus was twelve years old, he went with his parents to the Temple of Jerusalem. This episode fits into the context of pilgrimage, as St. Luke stresses: "His parents went to Jerusalem every year at the feast of the Passover. And when he was twelve years old, they went up according to custom" (2:41-42).

Pilgrimage is an expression of religious devotion that is nourished by and at the same time nourishes prayer. Here it is the Passover pilgrimage, and the Evangelist points out to us that the family of Jesus made this pilgrimage every year in order to take part in the rites in the holy city. Jewish families, like Christian families, pray in the intimacy of the home, but they also pray together with the community, recognizing that they belong to the People of God journeying on; and the pilgrimage expresses exactly this state of the People of God on the move. Easter is the center and culmination of all this and involves both the family dimension and that of liturgical and public worship.

In the episode of the twelve-year-old Jesus, his first words are also recorded: "How is it that you sought me? Did you not know that I must be in my Father's house?" (Luke 2:49). After three days spent looking for him, his parents found him in the Temple, sitting among the teachers, listening to them and asking them questions (cf. 2:46). His answer to the question of why he had done this to his father and mother was that he had only done what the Son should do, that is, to be with his Father.

Thus, he showed who the true Father is, what the true home is, and that he had done nothing unusual or disobedient. He had stayed where the Son ought to be, that is, with the Father, and he stressed who his Father was.

The term "Father," therefore, dominates the tone of this answer, and the Christological mystery appears in its entirety. Hence, this word unlocks the mystery: it is the key to the mystery of Christ, who is the Son, and also the key to our mystery as Christians, who are sons and daughters in the Son. At the same time, Jesus teaches us to be children by being with the Father in prayer. The Christological mystery, the mystery of Christian existence, is closely linked to—and founded on—prayer. Jesus was one day to teach his disciples to pray, telling them, "When you pray, say: 'Father'" (Luke 11:2). And naturally, do not just say the word; say it with your life, learn to say it meaningfully with your life—"Father"—and in this way you will be true sons in the Son, true Christians.

—General Audience, Paul VI Audience Hall, December 28, 2011

Remaining Ever United to Jesus

Jesus said to his disciples, "I am the true vine, and my Father is the vinedresser" (John 15:1). In the Bible, Israel is often compared to the fertile vine when it is faithful to God; but if it distances itself from him, it becomes barren, incapable of producing that "wine to gladden the heart of man," as Psalm 104 sings (verse 15). The true vine of God, true life, is Jesus, who with his sacrifice of love gives us salvation, opening to us the way to be part of this vine. And as Jesus remains in the love of God the Father, the disciples too, . . . if they remain profoundly united in him, become fruitful branches that bear an abundant harvest.

St. Francis de Sales wrote:

> The vine-sprig, united and joined to the stock, brings forth fruit not by its own power but in virtue of the stock. Now we are united by charity unto our Redeemer as members to their head, and hence it is that . . . good works, drawing their worth from him, merit life everlasting. (*Treatise on the Love of God*, XI, 6)

On the day of our baptism, the Church grafts us, as branches, onto the paschal mystery of Jesus, onto his very Person. From this root we receive the precious sap that enables us to share in the divine life. As disciples, with the help of the pastors of the Church, we, too, develop in the Lord's vineyard, bound by his love. "If the fruit we are to bear is love, its prerequisite is this 'remaining,' which is profoundly connected with the kind of faith that holds on to the Lord and does not let go" (Benedict XVI, *Jesus of Nazareth* [New York: Doubleday, 2007], 262).

It is indispensable to remain ever united to Jesus, to depend on him, because apart from him we can do nothing (cf. John 15:5). In a letter written to John the Prophet, who lived in the desert of Gaza in the fifth century, a faithful Christian asked the following question: How is it possible to combine man's freedom and the inability to do anything without God? And the monk answered: If man inclines his heart toward goodness and asks God for help, he receives the necessary strength to carry out his work. Therefore, man's freedom and God's power proceed together. This is possible because goodness comes from the Lord, but it is carried out through his faithful (cf. *Ep.* 763, collected in *Sources Chrétiennes*, 468 [Paris: Le Éditions du Cerf, 2002], 206).

True "abiding" in Christ guarantees the effectiveness of prayer, as the Cistercian Blessed Guerric of Igny said: "O Lord Jesus . . . without you we can do nothing. Indeed, you are the true gardener, creator, cultivator, and custodian of your garden, which you plan with your word, irrigate with your spirit and cause to grow with your power" (*Sermo ad excitandam devotionem in psalmodia,* collected in *Sources Chrétiennes* , 202 [Paris: Le Éditions du Cerf, 1973], 522).

Dear friends, each one of us is like a branch that lives only if its union with the Lord grows every day in prayer, in participation in the sacraments, and in charity. And he who loves Jesus, the true vine, produces fruits of faith for an abundant spiritual harvest. Let us pray to the Mother of God that we may remain firmly grafted onto Jesus and that all our actions may have their beginning and end in him.

—Regina Caeli Address, St. Peter's Square, May 6, 2012

The Prayer of Jesus in Gethsemane

"*Abba*, Father, all things are possible to you; remove this chalice from me; yet not what I will, but what you will" (Mark 14:36). In this invocation there are three revealing passages. At the beginning, we have the double use of the word with which Jesus addresses God: "*Abba*! Father!" We know well that the Aramaic word *Abbà* is the term that children use to address their father, and hence that it expresses Jesus' relationship with God: a relationship of tenderness, affection, trust, and abandonment.

The second element is found in the central part of the invocation. Awareness of the Father's omnipotence—"All things are possible to you"—introduces a request in which, once again, the drama of Jesus' human will appears as he faces death and evil: "Remove this chalice from me!"

However, there is the third expression in Jesus' prayer—and it is the crucial one—in which the human will adheres to the divine will without reserve. In fact, Jesus ends by saying forcefully, "Yet not what I will but what you will." In the unity of the Divine Person of the Son, the human will finds its complete fulfillment in the total abandonment of the "I" to the "You" of the Father, called *Abba*.

St. Maximus the Confessor says that ever since the moment of the creation of man and woman, the human will has been oriented to the divine will, and that it is precisely in the "yes" to God that the human will is fully free and finds its fulfillment. Unfortunately, because of sin, this "yes" to God is transformed into opposition: Adam and Eve thought that the "no" to God was the crowning point of freedom, of being fully themselves.

On the Mount of Olives, Jesus brings the human will back to the unreserved "yes" to God; in him the natural will is fully integrated in the orientation that the Divine Person gives it. Jesus lives his life in accordance with the center of his Person: his being the Son of God. His human will is drawn into the "I" of the Son who abandons himself totally to the Father. Thus, Jesus tells us that it is only by conforming our own will to the divine one that human beings attain their true height, that they become "divine"; only by coming out of ourselves, only in the "yes" to God, is Adam's desire, and the desire of us all, to be completely free. It is what Jesus brings about at Gethsemane: in transferring the human will into the divine will, the true man is born, and we are redeemed.

The *Compendium of the Catechism of the Catholic Church* teaches concisely:

> The prayer of Jesus during his agony in the Garden of Gethsemane and his last words on the cross reveal the depth of his filial prayer. Jesus brings to completion the loving plan of the Father and takes upon himself all the anguish of humanity and all the petitions and intercessions of the history of salvation. He presents them to the Father who accepts them and answers them beyond all hope by raising his Son from the dead. (543)

Truly, "nowhere else in Sacred Scripture do we gain so deep an insight into the inner mystery of Jesus as in the prayer on the

Mount of Olives" (Benedict XVI, *Jesus of Nazareth: Part Two* [San Francisco: Ignatius Press, 2011], 157).

Dear brothers and sisters, every day in the prayer of the Our Father, we ask the Lord, "Thy will be done, / On earth as it is in heaven" (Matthew 6:10). In other words, we recognize that there is a will of God with us and for us, a will of God for our life that must become every day, increasingly, the reference of our willing and of our being. We recognize, moreover, that "heaven" is where God's will is done and where the "earth" becomes "heaven"—a place where love, goodness, truth, and divine beauty are present—only if, on earth, God's will is done.

In Jesus' prayer to the Father on that terrible and marvelous night in Gethsemane, the "earth" became "heaven"; the "earth" of his human will, shaken by fear and anguish, was taken up by his divine will in such a way that God's will was done on earth. And this is also important in our own prayers: we must learn to entrust ourselves more to Divine Providence, to ask God for the strength to come out of ourselves in order to renew our "yes" to him, to say to him, "Thy will be done," so as to conform our will to his. It is a prayer we must pray every day because it is not always easy to entrust ourselves to God's will, repeating the "yes" of Jesus, the "yes" of Mary.

—General Audience, Paul VI Audience Hall, February 1, 2012

II

RESPONDING TO THE GOD OF LOVE

Lord, Help Us Recognize the Immensity of Your Love

In chapter three of the Letter to the Ephesians, St. Paul speaks to us of the need to be "strengthened . . . in the inner man" (verse 16). With this he takes up a subject that earlier, in a troubled situation, he had addressed in the Second Letter to the Corinthians: "Though our outer nature is wasting away, our inner nature is being renewed every day" (4:16). The inner person must be strengthened; this is a very appropriate imperative for our time, in which people all too often remain inwardly empty and must therefore cling to promises and drugs, which then results in a further growth of the sense of emptiness in their hearts. This interior void—the weakness of the inner person—is one of the great problems of our time. Interiority must be reinforced by the perceptiveness of the heart, the capacity to see and understand the world and the person from within, with one's heart. We are in need of reason illuminated by the heart in order to learn to act in accordance with the truth in love. However, this is not realized without an intimate relationship with God, without the life of prayer. We need the encounter with God that is given to us in the sacraments. And we cannot speak to God in prayer unless we let him speak first, unless we listen to him in the words that he has given us.

In this regard, Paul says to us:

> May Christ dwell in your hearts through faith; that you, being rooted and grounded in love, may have power to

comprehend with all the saints what is the breadth and length and height and depth, and to know the love of Christ which surpasses knowledge. (Ephesians 3:17-19)

With these words, Paul tells us that love sees beyond simple reason. And he also tells us that only in communion with all the saints, that is, in the great community of all believers and not against or without it, can we know the immensity of Christ's mystery. He circumscribes this immensity with words meant to express the dimensions of the cosmos: breadth, length, height, and depth. The mystery of Christ has a cosmic vastness; he did not belong only to a specific group. The crucified Christ embraces the entire universe in all its dimensions. He takes the world in his hands and lifts it up toward God. Starting with St. Irenaeus of Lyons—thus from the second century—the Fathers have seen in these words on the breadth, length, height, and depth of Christ's love an allusion to the cross. In the cross Christ's love embraced the lowest depths, the night of death, as well as the supreme heights, the loftiness of God himself. And he took into his arms the breadth and the vastness of humanity and of the world in all their distances. He always embraces the universe—all of us.

Let us pray to the Lord to help us to recognize something of the immensity of his love. Let us pray to him that his love and his truth may touch our hearts. Let us ask that Christ dwell in our hearts and make us new men and women who act according to truth in love. Amen!

—Homily, Basilica of St. Paul Outside-the-Walls, June 28, 2009

In Love We Go Toward God

St. Paul says that God himself has made a sacrifice: he has given us his own Son; he gave him on the cross to triumph over sin and death, to triumph over the evil one, and to overcome all the evil that exists in the world. And God's extraordinary mercy inspires the apostle's admiration and profound trust in the power of God's love for us. Indeed, St. Paul says, "He [God] who did not spare his own Son but gave him up for us all, will he not also give us all things with him?" (Romans 8:32).

If God gives himself in the Son, he gives us everything. And Paul insists on the power of Christ's redeeming sacrifice against every other force that can threaten our life. He wonders: "Who shall bring any charge against God's elect? It is God who justifies; who is to condemn? Is it Christ Jesus, who died, yes, who was raised from the dead, who is at the right hand of God, who indeed intercedes for us?" (Romans 8:33-34).

We are in God's heart—this is our great trust. This creates love, and in love we go toward God. If God has given his own Son for all of us, no one can accuse us, no one can condemn us, no one can separate us from his immense love. Precisely the supreme sacrifice of love on the cross, which the Son of God accepted and chose willingly, becomes the source of our justification, of our salvation. Just think that this act of the Lord's endures in the Blessed Eucharist, and in his heart, for eternity, and this act of love attracts us, unites us with him.

—Homily, Torino, March 4, 2012

THE LOVING FACE OF GOD

"God so loved the world that he gave his only-begotten Son" (John 3:16). This is one of the central verses of the gospel. The subject is God the Father, origin of the whole creating and redeeming mystery. The verbs "to love" and "to give" indicate a decisive and definitive act that expresses the radicalism with which God approached man in love, even to the total gift of crossing the threshold of our ultimate solitude, throwing himself into the abyss of our extreme abandonment, going beyond the door of death. The object and beneficiary of divine love is the world, namely, humanity. It is a word that erases completely the idea of a distant God alien to man's journey and reveals, rather, his true face. He gave us his Son out of love, to be the God who is near, to make us feel his presence, to come to meet us and carry us in his love so that the whole of life might be enlivened by this divine love. The Son of Man did not come to be served but to serve and to give life.

God does not domineer but loves without measure. He does not express his omnipotence in punishment but in mercy and in forgiveness. Understanding all this means entering into the mystery of salvation. Jesus came to save, not to condemn; with the sacrifice of the cross, he reveals the loving face of God. Precisely by faith in the abundant love that has been given to us in Christ Jesus, we know that even the smallest force of love is greater than the greatest destructive force and can transform the world, and by this same faith we can have the "reliable hope," in eternal life and in the resurrection of the flesh.

—Homily, St. Peter's Basilica, November 4, 2010

ARE WE STILL WAITING FOR A SAVIOR?

It was out of love that the Creator of the universe came to dwell among us. In his Letter to the Philippians, St. Paul says that Christ, "though he was in the form of God, did not count equality with God a thing to be grasped, but emptied himself, taking the form of a servant, being born in the likeness of men" (2:6-7). He appeared in human form, adds the apostle, humbling himself. . . . St. Paul says further, "When the time had fully come, God sent forth his Son, born of woman, born under the law, to redeem those who were under the law, so that we might receive adoption as sons" (Galatians 4:4-5). In truth, the chosen people had been waiting for the Messiah for many centuries, but they imagined him as a powerful and victorious army leader who would free his followers from foreign oppression.

The Savior, on the contrary, was born in silence and in absolute poverty. He came as "the light that enlightens every man," St. John notes, yet "his own people received him not" (John 1:9, 11). "But," the apostle adds, "to all who received him, who believed in his name, he gave power to become children of

God" (1:12). The light promised was to illumine the hearts of those who had persevered in vigilant and active expectation. . . .

But the question is: Is the humanity of our time still waiting for a Savior? One has the feeling that many consider God as foreign to their own interests. Apparently, they do not need him. They live as though he did not exist and, worse still, as though he were an "obstacle" to remove in order to fulfill themselves. Even among believers—we are sure of it—some let themselves be attracted by enticing dreams and distracted by misleading doctrines that suggest deceptive shortcuts to happiness.

Yet despite its contradictions, worries, and tragedies, and perhaps precisely because of them, humanity today seeks a path of renewal, of salvation; it seeks a Savior and awaits, sometimes unconsciously, the coming of the Savior who renews the world and our life, the coming of Christ, the one true Redeemer of man and of the whole of man.

—General Audience, Paul VI Audience Hall, December 20, 2006

WE MUST BE REBORN AS CHILDREN OF GOD

I would like to offer a brief reflection on the fact that we are children of God. First of all, however, let us start with our being, quite simply, children: this is the fundamental condition that brings us all together. We are not all parents, but we are certainly all children.

Being born is never a choice; we are not asked first whether we wish to be born. Yet in life we can develop a free attitude with regard to life itself: we can regard it as a gift and, in a certain sense, "become" what we are—children. This transition marks a turning point of maturity in our existence and in our relationship with our parents, which is filled with gratitude. It is a transition that also renders us capable, in turn, of being parents, not biologically, but morally.

Also before God we are all children. God is at the root of every created being's life and is the Father of every human person in a special way: he has a unique and personal relationship with every human being. Each one of us is wanted and loved by God. And also in this relationship with God, we can be "reborn," so to speak; in other words, we become what we are. This happens through faith, through a profound and personal "yes" to God as the origin and foundation of our existence. With this "yes" I receive life as a gift of the Father who is in heaven, a Parent whom I do not see but in whom I believe and whom, in the depths of my heart, I feel is my Father and the Father of all my brethren in humanity, an immensely good and faithful Father.

On what is this faith in God the Father based? It is based on Jesus Christ: he himself and his history reveal the Father to us, enabling us to know him as much as is possible in this world. Believing that Jesus is the Christ, the Son of God, makes it possible to be "born from above," that is, from God, who is love (cf. John 3:3).

Moreover, let us bear in mind once again that no individual makes himself or herself a human being. We are born without doing anything ourselves; the *passivity* of being born precedes the *activity* of what we ourselves do. It is also the same at the level of being Christian: no one can become Christian solely by one's own will. Being Christian is also a gift that comes before our own action: we must be reborn in a new birth. St. John says, "To all who received him, . . . he gave power to become children of God" (John 1:12).

This is the meaning of the Sacrament of Baptism. Baptism is this new birth that precedes our own action. With our faith we can go to meet Christ, but he alone can make us Christian and give to our will and to this desire of ours the response, dignity, and power to become children of God, which we ourselves do not possess.

. . . Let us give thanks to God for this great mystery, which is a source of regeneration for the Church and for the whole world. God made himself the Son of Man so that man might become a son of God. Let us therefore renew our joy in being children, as men and women and as Christians, *born* and *reborn* to a new divine existence—born from the love of a father and a mother, and reborn from the love of God through baptism.

Let us ask the Virgin Mary, Mother of Christ, and of all who believe in him, to help us to live truly as children of God, not in words, or not only in words, but with deeds. St. John writes further, "This is his commandment, that we should believe in the name of his Son Jesus Christ and love one another, just as he has commanded us" (1 John 3:23).

—Angelus Address, St. Peter's Square, January 8, 2012

Standing on the Safest Rock

Our radical belonging to Christ and the fact that "we are in him" must imbue in us an attitude of total trust and immense joy. In short, we must indeed exclaim with St. Paul, "If God is for us, who is against us?" (Romans 8:31). And the reply is that nothing and no one "will be able to separate us from the love of God in Christ Jesus our Lord" (8:39). Our Christian life, therefore, stands on the soundest and safest rock one can imagine. And from it we draw all our energy, precisely as the apostle wrote, "I can do all things in him who strengthens me" (Philippians 4:13).

Therefore, let us face our life with its joys and sorrows supported by these great sentiments that Paul offers to us. By having an experience of them, we will realize how true are the words the apostle himself wrote: "I know whom I have believed, and I am sure that he is able to guard until that Day what has been entrusted to me" (2 Timothy 1:12); in other words, until the day of our definitive meeting with Christ the Judge, Savior of the world, and our Savior.

—General Audience, St. Peter's Square, November 8, 2006

Love Is the Reason for the Incarnation

God comes to dwell among us; he comes for us, to remain with us. A question passes through these two thousand years of Christian history: "But why did he do it, why did God become man? . . . Why did God make himself man?" St. Irenaeus writes: "The Word made himself dispenser of the Father's glory for the benefit of men. . . . The glory of God is the living man—*vivens homo*—and the life of man consists in the vision of God" (*Adversus Haereses* 20:5, 7).

The glory of God is manifest, therefore, in the salvation of man, whom God so loved as "to give," as the Evangelist John affirms, "his only Son, that whoever believes in him should not perish but have eternal life" (John 3:16).

Hence, love is the ultimate reason for the Incarnation of Christ.

In this regard, the reflection of the theologian Hans Urs von Balthasar is eloquent. He wrote, God "is not, in the first place, absolute power, but absolute love, whose sovereignty is not manifest in keeping for himself what belongs to him, but in his abandonment" (*Mysterium Paschale* [Leipzig: St. Benno-Verlag, 1970], I, 4). The God we contemplate in the crib is God-Love.

—General Audience, Paul VI Audience Hall, December 27, 2006

LOVE GIVES JOYFULLY

In this Gospel account [John 12:1-11], there is one gesture to which I would like to draw attention. Mary of Bethany "took a pound of costly ointment of pure nard and anointed the feet of Jesus and wiped his feet with her hair" (12:3). Mary's gesture is the expression of great faith and love for the Lord. It is not enough for her to wash the Teacher's feet with water; she sprinkles on them a great quantity of the precious perfume, which, as Judas protested, would have been possible to sell for three hundred denarii. She does not anoint his head, as was the custom, but his feet. Mary offers Jesus the most precious thing she has and with a gesture of deep devotion. Love does not calculate, does not measure, does not worry about expense, does not set up barriers, but can give joyfully; it seeks only the good of the other and surmounts meanness, pettiness, resentment, and the narrow-mindedness that human beings sometimes harbor in their hearts.

Mary stood at the feet of Jesus in a humble attitude of service, the same attitude that the Teacher himself was to assume at the Last Supper when . . . [he] "began to wash the disciples' feet" (John 13:5) and said, "You also should do as I have done to you" (13:15). The rule of the community of Jesus is that of love that knows how to serve to the point of offering one's life. And the scent spread: "the house" the Evangelist remarks, "was filled with the fragrance of the ointment" (12:3). The meaning of Mary's action, which is a response to God's infinite love, spreads among all the guests: no gesture of charity and authentic devotion to Christ remains a personal event or concerns solely the relationship between the individual and the Lord. Rather, it concerns the whole body of the Church; it is contagious: it instills love, joy, and light. . . .

In the sermon in which he comments on this Gospel passage, St. Augustine addresses each one of us with insistent words the invitation to enter this circuit of love by imitating Mary's gesture and really placing ourselves in the presence of Christ. Augustine writes:

> Whatever soul of you wishes to be truly faithful, anoint like Mary the feet of the Lord with precious ointment. . . . Anoint the feet of Jesus: follow by a good life the Lord's footsteps. Wipe them with your hair: what you have of superfluity, give to the poor, and then you have wiped the feet of the Lord. (*In Johannis evangelium tractatus* 50, 6)

—Homily, St. Peter's Basilica, March 29, 2010

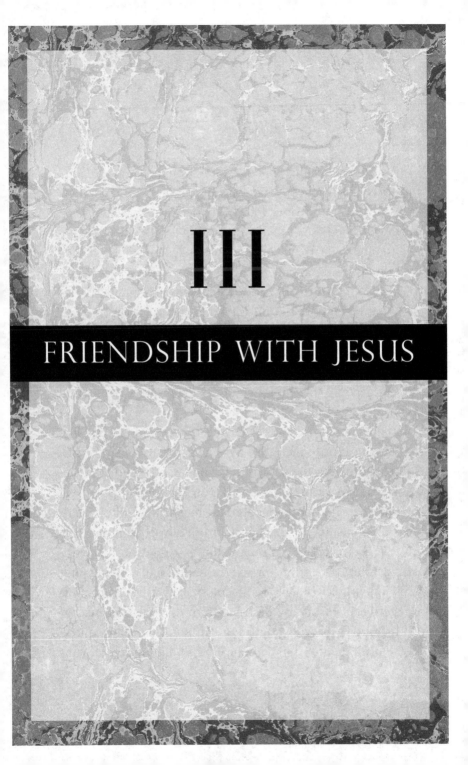

III

FRIENDSHIP WITH JESUS

Let Us Become Friends of Jesus

"This is eternal life, that they may know you the only true God, and Jesus Christ whom you have sent" (John 17:3). Everyone wants to have life. We long for a life that is authentic, complete, worthwhile, and full of joy. This yearning for life coexists with a resistance to death, which nonetheless remains inescapable. When Jesus speaks about eternal life, he is referring to real and true life, a life worthy of being lived. He is not simply speaking about life after death. He is talking about authentic life, a life fully alive and thus not subject to death, yet one which can already, and indeed must, begin in this world. Only if we learn even now how to live authentically, if we learn how to live the life that death cannot take away, does the promise of eternity become meaningful.

But how does this happen? What is this true and eternal life that death cannot touch? We have heard Jesus' answer: this is eternal life, that they may know you—God—and the One whom you have sent, Jesus Christ. Much to our surprise, we are told that life is knowledge. This means, first of all, that life is relationship. No one has life from himself and only for himself. We have it from others and in a relationship with others. If it is a relationship in truth and love, a giving and receiving, it gives fullness to life and makes it beautiful. But for that very reason, the destruction of that relationship by death can be especially painful; it can put life itself in question. Only a relationship with the One who is himself life can preserve my life beyond the floodwaters of death, can bring me through them alive.

Already in Greek philosophy, we encounter the idea that man can find eternal life if he clings to what is indestructible— to truth, which is eternal. He needs, as it were, to be full of truth in order to bear within himself the stuff of eternity. But only if truth is a Person can it lead me through the night of death. We cling to God—to Jesus Christ, the risen One. And thus we are led by the One who is himself life. In this relationship we, too, live by passing through death, since we are not forsaken by the One who is himself life.

But let us return to Jesus' words—this is eternal life: that they know you and the One whom you have sent. Knowledge of God becomes eternal life. Clearly, "knowledge" here means something more than mere factual knowledge, as, for example, when we know that a famous person has died or a discovery has been made. Knowing, in the language of Sacred Scripture, is an interior becoming one with the other. Knowing God, knowing Christ, always means loving him, becoming, in a sense, one with him by virtue of that knowledge and love. Our life becomes authentic and true life, and thus eternal life, when we know the One who is the source of all being and all life. And so Jesus' words become a summons: let us become friends of Jesus, let us try to know him all the more! Let us live in dialogue with him! Let us learn from him how to live aright, let us be his witnesses! Then we become people who love, and then we act aright. Then we are truly alive.

—Homily, Holy Thursday, St. Peter's Basilica, April 1, 2010

NONE ARE EXCLUDED FROM JESUS' FRIENDSHIP

Jesus welcomes into the group of his close friends a man who, according to the concepts in vogue in Israel at that time, was regarded as a public sinner.

Matthew, in fact, not only handled money deemed impure because of its provenance from people foreign to the People of God, but he also collaborated with an alien and despicably greedy authority whose tributes, moreover, could be arbitrarily determined. This is why the Gospels several times link "tax collectors and sinners" (Matthew 9:10; Luke 15:1), as well as "tax collectors and harlots " (Matthew 21:31). Furthermore, the Gospels see publicans as an example of miserliness (cf. 5:46: they only like those who like them), and mention one of them, Zacchaeus, as "a chief tax collector, and rich" (Luke 19:2). Popular opinion associated them with "extortioners, the unjust, adulterers" (18:11).

A first fact strikes one based on these references: Jesus does not exclude anyone from his friendship. Indeed, precisely while he is at table in the home of Matthew-Levi, in response to those who expressed shock at the fact that he associated with people who had so little to recommend them, he made this important statement: "Those who are well have no need of a physician, but those who are sick; I came not to call the righteous, but sinners" (Mark 2:17).

The good news of the gospel consists precisely in this: offering God's grace to the sinner!

Elsewhere, with the famous words of the Pharisee and the publican who went up to the Temple to pray, Jesus actually indicates an anonymous tax collector as an appreciated example of humble trust in divine mercy: while the Pharisee is boasting of his own moral perfection, the "tax collector . . . would not even lift up his eyes to heaven, but beat his breast, saying, 'God, be merciful to me a sinner!'"

And Jesus comments, "I tell you, this man went down to his house justified rather than the other; for every one who exalts himself will be humbled, but he who humbles himself will be exalted" (Luke 18:13-14).

Thus, in the figure of Matthew, the Gospels present to us a true and proper paradox: those who seem to be the farthest from holiness can even become a model of the acceptance of God's mercy and offer a glimpse of its marvelous effects in their own lives.

—General Audience, Paul VI Audience Hall, August 30, 2006

The Joy of Being Visited by the Son of God

The Evangelist St. Luke pays special attention to the theme of Jesus' mercy. In fact, in his narration we find some episodes that highlight the merciful love of God and of Christ, who said that he had come to call not the just but sinners (cf. Luke 5:32).

Among Luke's typical accounts, there is that of the conversion of Zacchaeus [19:1-10]. . . .

Zacchaeus is a publican; indeed, he is the head of the publicans of Jericho, an important city on the River Jordan. The publicans were the tax collectors who collected the tribute that the Jews had to pay to the Roman emperor, and already for this reason, they were considered public sinners. What is more, they often took advantage of their position to extort money from the people. Because of this, Zacchaeus was very rich but despised by his fellow citizens. So when Jesus was passing through Jericho and stopped at the house of Zacchaeus, he caused a general scandal. The Lord, however, knew exactly what he was doing. He wanted, so to speak, to gamble, and he won the bet: Zacchaeus, deeply moved by Jesus' visit, decided to change his life and promised to restore four times what he had stolen. "Today salvation has come to this house," Jesus says, and concludes, "The Son of man came to seek and to save the lost" (Luke 19:9-10).

God excludes no one, neither the poor nor the rich. God does not let himself be conditioned by our human prejudices, but sees in everyone a soul to save, and is especially attracted to those who are judged as lost and who think themselves so. Jesus Christ, the Incarnation of God, has demonstrated this immense mercy, which takes nothing away from the gravity of sin but aims always at saving the sinner, at offering him the possibility of redemption, of starting again from the beginning, of converting.

In another passage of the Gospels, Jesus states that it is very difficult for a rich man to enter the kingdom of heaven (cf. Matthew 19:23). In the case of Zacchaeus, we see that precisely what seems impossible actually happens: "He," St. Jerome comments, "gave away his wealth and immediately replaced it with the wealth of the kingdom of heaven" (*Homily on Psalm 83:3*). And St. Maximus of Turin adds, "Riches, for the foolish, feed dishonesty, but for the wise they are a help to virtue; for the latter they offer a chance of salvation, for the former they procure a stumbling block and perdition" (*Sermon 95*).

Dear friends, Zacchaeus welcomed Jesus, and he converted because Jesus first welcomed him! He did not condemn him, but he met his desire for salvation. Let us pray to the Virgin Mary, perfect model of communion with Jesus, to be renewed by his love so that we, too, may experience the joy of being visited by the Son of God, of being renewed by his love, and of transmitting his mercy to others.

—Angelus Address, St. Peter's Square, October 31, 2010

KNOWING JESUS THROUGH AN INTENSE RELATIONSHIP

The Gospel we have just heard (cf. Matthew 16:13-20) suggests two different ways of knowing Christ. The first is an impersonal knowledge, one based on current opinion. When Jesus asks, "Who do people say that the Son of Man is?" the disciples answer, "Some say John the Baptist, others Elijah, still others Jeremiah or one of the prophets" (16:13-14, NAB). In other words, Christ is seen as yet another religious figure, like those who came before him. Then Jesus turns to the disciples and asks them, "But who do you say that I am?" (16:15, NAB). Peter responds with what is the first confession of faith: "You are the Messiah, the Son of the living God" (16:16, NAB). Faith is more than just empirical or historical facts; it is an ability to grasp the mystery of Christ's person in all its depth.

Yet faith is not the result of human effort, of human reasoning, but rather a gift of God: "Blessed are you, Simon son of Jonah. For flesh and blood has not revealed this to you, but my heavenly Father" (Matthew 16:17, NAB). Faith starts with God, who opens his heart to us and invites us to share in his own divine life. Faith does not simply provide information about who Christ is; rather, it entails a personal relationship with Christ, a surrender of our whole person, with all our understanding, will, and feelings, to God's self-revelation. So Jesus' question—"But who do you say that I am?"—is ultimately a challenge to the disciples to make a personal decision in his regard. Faith in Christ and discipleship are tightly interconnected.

And since faith involves following the Master, it must become constantly stronger, deeper, and more mature to the extent that it leads to a closer and more intense relationship with Jesus. Peter and the other disciples also had to grow in this way, until their encounter with the risen Lord opened their eyes to the fullness of faith.

Dear young people, today Christ is asking you the same question that he asked the apostles: "Who do you say that I am?" Respond to him with generosity and courage, as befits young hearts like your own. Say to him: "Jesus, I know that you are the Son of God who has given your life for me. I want to follow you faithfully and to be led by your word. You know me, and you love me. I place my trust in you, and I put my whole life into your hands. I want you to be the power that strengthens me and the joy that never leaves me."

—Address, 26th World Youth Day, Madrid, August 21, 2011

Contemplating the Face of Jesus

During the Last Supper, after Jesus affirmed that to know him was also to know the Father (cf. John 14:7), Philip quite ingenuously asks him, "Lord, show us the Father, and we shall be satisfied" (14:8). Jesus answered with a gentle rebuke:

> "Have I been with you so long, and yet you do not know me, Philip? He who has seen me has seen the Father; how can you say, 'Show us the Father'? Do you not believe that I am in the Father and the Father is in me? . . . Believe me that I am in the Father and the Father is in me." (14:9-11)

These words are among the most exalted in John's Gospel. They contain a true and proper revelation. At the end of the prologue to his Gospel, John says, "No one has ever seen God; the only Son, who is in the bosom of the Father, he has made him known" (1:18).

Well, that declaration, which is made by the Evangelist, is taken up and confirmed by Jesus himself but with a fresh nuance. In fact, whereas John's prologue speaks of an explanatory intervention by Jesus through the words of his teaching, in his answer to Philip, Jesus refers to his own Person as such, letting it be understood that it is possible to understand him not only through his words but, rather, simply through what he is.

To express ourselves in accordance with the paradox of the Incarnation, we can certainly say that God gave himself a human face, the face of Jesus, and consequently, from now on, if we truly want to know the face of God, all we have to do is to contemplate the face of Jesus! In his face we truly see who God is and what he looks like!

The Evangelist does not tell us whether Philip grasped the full meaning of Jesus' sentence. There is no doubt that he dedicated his whole life entirely to him. According to certain later accounts (Acts of Philip and others), our apostle is said to have evangelized first Greece and then Frisia, where he is supposed to have died—in Hierapolis—by a torture described variously as crucifixion or stoning.

Let us conclude our reflection by recalling the aim to which our whole life must aspire: to encounter Jesus as Philip encountered him, seeking to perceive in him God himself, the heavenly Father. If this commitment were lacking, we would be reflected back to ourselves as in a mirror and become more and more lonely! Philip teaches us instead to let ourselves be won over by Jesus, to be with him, and also to invite others to share in this indispensable company; and in seeing and finding God, to find true life.

—General Audience, St. Peter's Square, September 6, 2006

I Have Seen the Lord!

St. Augustine recalled incisively:

> Let us consider, dear friends, the resurrection of Christ: indeed, just as his passion stood for our old life, his resurrection is a sacrament of new life. . . . You have believed, you have been baptized; the old life is dead, killed on the cross, buried in baptism. The old life in which you lived is buried: the new life emerges. Live well: live life in such a way that when death comes, you will not die. (*Sermo Guelferb* 9, 3)

The Gospel accounts that mention the appearances of the risen One usually end with the invitation to overcome every uncertainty, to confront the event with the Scriptures, to proclaim that Jesus, beyond death, is alive forever, a source of new life for all who believe in him.

This is what happened, for example, in the case of Mary Magdalene (cf. John 20:11-18), who found the tomb open and empty and immediately feared that the body of the Lord had been taken away. The Lord then called her by name, and at that point, a deep change took place within her: her distress and bewilderment were transformed into joy and enthusiasm. She promptly went to the apostles and announced to them, "I have seen the Lord" (20:18).

Behold: those who meet the risen Jesus are inwardly transformed; it is impossible *"to see"* the risen One without *"believing"* in him. Let us pray that he will call each one of us by name and thus convert us, opening us to the *"vision"* of faith.

Faith is born from the personal encounter with the risen Christ and becomes an impulse of courage and freedom that makes one cry to the world: "Jesus is risen and alive forever."

This is the mission of the Lord's disciples in every epoch and also in our time: "If then you have been raised with Christ," St. Paul exhorts us, "seek the things that are above. . . . Set your minds on things that are above, not on things that are on earth" (Colossians 3:1-2). This does not mean cutting oneself off from one's daily commitments, neglecting earthly realities; rather, it means reviving every human activity with a supernatural breath, it means making ourselves joyful proclaimers and witnesses of the resurrection of Christ, living for eternity (cf. John 20:25; Luke 24:33-34).

—General Audience, St. Peter's Square, April 19, 2006

The Risen Jesus Is Present in Our Midst

In this catechesis I would like to demonstrate the transformation that the Pasch of Jesus worked in his disciples. Let us start with the evening of the day of the resurrection. The disciples had locked the door to the house for fear of the Jews (cf. John 20:19). Fear caused their hearts to miss a beat and prevented them from reaching out to others and to life. The Teacher was no longer. The memory of his passion gave rise to uncertainty. Yet Jesus had his followers at heart and was about to fulfill the promise he had made during the Last Supper: "I will not leave you desolate; I will come to you" (14:18), and he also says this to us: "I will not leave you desolate."

With Jesus' arrival, the disciples' feelings of anguish change radically. He enters through closed doors; he stands in their midst and gives them the peace that reassures: "Peace be with you" (John 20:19b). It is a common greeting, but it now acquires new significance because it brings about an inner change; it is the Easter greeting that enables the disciples to overcome all fear. The peace that Jesus brings is the gift of salvation that he had promised in his farewell discourses: "Peace I leave with you; my peace I give to you; not as the world gives do I give to you. Let not your hearts be troubled, neither let them be afraid" (14:27).

On this day of the resurrection, he gives it in fullness, and for the community it becomes a source of joy, the certainty of victory, and security in relying on God. "Let not your hearts be troubled" (John 14:1); "Do not be afraid," he also says to us.

After this greeting, Jesus shows the disciples the wounds in his hands and in his side (cf. John 20:20)—signs of what has occurred and will never be cancelled: his glorious humanity remains "wounded." The purpose of this act is to confirm the new reality of the resurrection: Christ, now among his own disciples, is a real Person, the same Jesus who three days earlier was nailed to the cross. And it is in this way, in the dazzling light of Easter, in the encounter with the risen One, that the disciples perceive the salvific meaning of his passion and his death. Then sorrow and fear turn into full joy. The sorrow and the wounds themselves become a source of joy.

The joy that is born in their hearts derives from "[having seen] the Lord" (John 20:20). He repeats to them, "Peace be with you" (20:21). By then it was obvious that it was not only a greeting. It was a gift, *the* gift that the risen One wants to offer his friends, but at the same time, it is a consignment. This peace, which Christ purchased with his blood, is for them but also for all, which the disciples must pass on to the whole world. Indeed, he adds, "As the Father has sent me, even so I send you" (20:21). The risen Jesus returned to his disciples to send them out. He had completed his work in the world; it was then up to them to sow faith in hearts so that the Father, known and loved, might gather all his children from the dispersion.

But Jesus knows that his followers are still fearful, even now. Thus, he carries out the gesture of blowing upon them and regenerates them in his Spirit (cf. John 20:22); this action is the sign of the new creation. In fact, with the gift of the Holy Spirit that comes from the risen Christ, a new world begins. The sending of the disciples on mission is the beginning of the journey in the world of the people of the new covenant, a people who believe in him and in his work of salvation, a people who witness to the truth of the resurrection. This newness of life that does not die, brought by Easter, must be spread everywhere so that the thorns of sin, which wound the human heart, leave room for the new shoots of grace, of God's presence and of his love that triumph over sin and death.

Dear friends, today too the risen One enters our homes and our hearts, even when, at times, the doors are closed. He enters giving joy and peace, life and hope, gifts we need for our human and spiritual rebirth. Only he can roll away those stones from the tombs in which all too often people seal themselves off from their own feelings, their own relationships, their own behavior; stones that sanction death—division, enmity, resentment, envy, diffidence, indifference. Only he, the living One, can give meaning to existence. . . .

To conclude, the experience of the disciples invites us to think about the meaning of Easter for us. Let us allow ourselves to encounter the risen Jesus! He, alive and true, is ever present in our midst; he walks with us to guide our life, to open our eyes. Let us trust in the risen One, who has the power to give life, to make us be born anew as children of God, capable of believing and of loving. Faith in him transforms our life: frees it from fear, gives it firm hope, enlivens it with God's love, which gives full meaning to existence.

—General Audience, St. Peter's Square, April 11, 2012

Doubt That Leads to Faith

The proverbial scene of the doubting Thomas that occurred eight days after Easter is very well-known. At first he did not believe that Jesus had appeared in his absence and said, "Unless I see in his hands the print of the nails, and place my finger in the mark of the nails, and place my hand in his side, I will not believe" (John 20:25).

Basically, from these words emerges the conviction that Jesus can now be recognized by his wounds rather than by his face. Thomas holds that the signs that confirm Jesus' identity are now above all his wounds, in which he reveals to us how much he loved us. In this the apostle is not mistaken.

As we know, Jesus reappeared among his disciples eight days later, and this time Thomas was present. Jesus summons him: "Put your finger here, and see my hands; and put out your hand, and place it in my side; do not be faithless, but believing" (John 20:27).

Thomas reacts with the most splendid profession of faith in the whole of the New Testament: "My Lord and my God!" (John 20:28). St. Augustine comments on this: Thomas "saw and touched the man, and acknowledged the God whom he neither saw nor touched; but by the means of what he saw and touched, he now put far away from him every doubt, and believed the other" (*In Johannis evangelium tractatus* 121, 5).

The Evangelist continues with Jesus' last words to Thomas: "Have you believed because you have seen me? Blessed are those who have not seen and yet believe" (John 20:29). This sentence can also be put into the present: "Blessed are those who do not see and yet believe." In any case, here Jesus spells out a fundamental principle for Christians who will come after Thomas—hence, for all of us.

It is interesting to note that another Thomas, the great medieval theologian of Aquinas, juxtaposed this formula of blessedness with the apparently opposite one recorded by Luke: "Blessed are the eyes which see what you see!" (Luke 10:23). However, Aquinas comments, "Those who believe without seeing are more meritorious than those who, seeing, believe" (*In Johannis* XX, *lectio* VI 2566).

In fact, the Letter to the Hebrews, recalling the whole series of the ancient biblical patriarchs who believed in God without seeing the fulfillment of his promises, defines faith as "the assurance of things hoped for, the conviction of things not seen" (11:1).

The apostle Thomas's case is important to us for at least three reasons: first, because it comforts us in our insecurity; second, because it shows us that every doubt can lead to an outcome brighter than any uncertainty; and lastly, because the words that Jesus addressed to him remind us of the true meaning of mature faith and encourage us to persevere, despite the difficulty, along our journey of adherence to him.

—General Audience, St. Peter's Square, September 27, 2006

Jesus Adapts Himself to Our Weakness

The school of faith is not a triumphal march but a journey marked daily by suffering and love, trials and faithfulness. Peter, who promised absolute fidelity, knew the bitterness and humiliation of denial: the arrogant man learns the costly lesson of humility. Peter, too, must learn that he is weak and in need of forgiveness. Once his attitude changes and he understands the truth of his weak heart of a believing sinner, he weeps in a fit of liberating repentance. After this weeping, he is finally ready for his mission.

On a spring morning, this mission will be entrusted to him by the risen Christ. The encounter takes place on the shore of the Lake of Tiberias. John the Evangelist recounts the conversation between Jesus and Peter in that circumstance. There is a very significant play on words.

In Greek the word *phileo* means the love of friendship, tender but not all-encompassing; instead, the word *agapao* means love without reserve, total and unconditional. Jesus asks Peter the first time, "Simon, . . . do you love me (*agapas-me*)" with this total and unconditional love? (John 21:15).

Prior to the experience of betrayal, the apostle certainly would have said, "I love you (*agapo-se*) unconditionally." Now that he has known the bitter sadness of infidelity, the drama of his own weakness, he says with humility, "Lord, you know that I love you (*philo-se*)," that is, "I love you with my poor human love." Christ insists, "Simon, do you love me with this total love that

I want?" And Peter repeats the response of his humble human love: *"Kyrie, philo-se,"* "Lord, I love you as I am able to love you." The third time Jesus only says to Simon, *"Phileis-me?"* "Do you love me?"

Simon understands that his poor love is enough for Jesus; it is the only one of which he is capable. Nonetheless, he is grieved that the Lord spoke to him in this way. He thus replies, "Lord, you know everything; you know that I love you (*philose*)" (John 20:17).

This is to say that Jesus has put himself on the level of Peter, rather than Peter on Jesus' level! It is exactly this divine conformity that gives hope to the disciple, who experienced the pain of infidelity.

From here is born the trust that makes him able to follow Christ to the end: "This he said to show by what death he was to glorify God. And after this he said to him, 'Follow me'" (John 21:19).

From that day, Peter "followed" the Master with the precise awareness of his own fragility, but this understanding did not discourage him. Indeed, he knew that he could count on the presence of the risen One beside him.

From the naïve enthusiasm of initial acceptance, passing though the sorrowful experience of denial and the weeping of conversion, Peter succeeded in entrusting himself to that Jesus who adapted himself to his poor capacity of love. And in this way he shows us the way, notwithstanding all of our weakness. We know that Jesus adapts himself to this weakness of ours.

We follow him with our poor capacity to love, and we know that Jesus is good, and he accepts us. It was a long journey for Peter that made him a trustworthy witness, "rock" of the Church, because he was constantly open to the action of the Spirit of Jesus. Peter qualifies himself as a "witness of the sufferings of Christ as well as a partaker in the glory that is to be revealed" (1 Peter 5:1). When he was to write these words, he would already be elderly, heading toward the end of his life that would be sealed with martyrdom. He would then be ready to describe true joy and to indicate where it can be drawn from: the source is believing in and loving Christ with our weak but sincere faith, notwithstanding our fragility.

He would therefore write to the Christians of his community, and says also to us: "Without having seen him you love him; though you do not now see him you believe in him and rejoice with unutterable and exalted joy. As the outcome of your faith you obtain the salvation of your souls" (1 Peter 1:8-9).

—General Audience, St. Peter's Square, May 24, 2006

IV

LORD, TEACH US TO PRAY!

ɔN: MAKING CONTACT
ʜE HEART OF GOD

I want to speak of only one small aspect of the life of prayer—which is life in contact with God—namely, meditation. And what is meditation? It means "remembering" all that God has done and not forgetting his many great benefits (cf. Psalm 103:2b).

We often see only the negative things; we must also keep in mind all that is positive, the gifts that God has given us; we must be attentive to the positive signs that come from God and must remember them. Let us therefore speak of a type of prayer that in the Christian tradition is known as "mental prayer." We are usually familiar with vocal prayer.

The heart and the mind must, of course, take part in this prayer. However, we are speaking today of a meditation that does not consist of words but rather is a way of making contact with the heart of God in our mind. And here Mary is a very real model. Luke the Evangelist repeated several times that Mary "kept all these things, pondering them in her heart" (2:19; cf. 2:51b). As a good custodian, she did not forget; she was attentive to all that the Lord told her and did for her, and she meditated. In other words, she considered various things, pondering them in her heart.

Therefore, she who "believed" in the announcement of the angel [cf. Luke 1:45] and made herself the means of enabling the eternal Word of the Most High to become incarnate also welcomed in her heart the wonderful miracle of that human-divine birth. She meditated on it and paused to reflect on what God

was working within her in order to welcome the divine ~
her life and respond to it. The mystery of the Incarnation of ~
Son of God and of Mary's motherhood is of such magnitude that
it requires interiorization. It is not only something physical that
God brought about within her but is something that demanded
interiorization on the part of Mary, who endeavored to deepen
her understanding of it, to interpret its meaning, and to comprehend its consequences and implications.

Thus, day after day, in the silence of ordinary life, Mary
continued to treasure in her heart the sequence of marvelous
events that she witnessed until the supreme test of the cross and
the glory of the resurrection. Mary lived her life to the full—
her daily duties, her role as a mother—but she knew how to
reserve an inner space to reflect on the word and will of God,
on what was occurring within her, and on the mysteries of the
life of her Son.

In our time, we are taken up with so many activities and
duties, worries and problems. We often tend to fill all of the
spaces of the day without leaving a moment to pause and reflect
and to nourish our spiritual life, [which is] contact with God.

Mary teaches us how necessary it is to find in our busy day
moments for silent recollection, to meditate on what the Lord
wants to teach us, on how he is present and active in the world
and in our life—to be able to stop for a moment and meditate.
St. Augustine compares meditation on the mysteries of God to
the assimilation of food, and uses a verb that recurs throughout
the Christian tradition: "to ruminate"; that is, the mysteries of
God should continually resonate within us so that they become

lives, and nourish us as does the food

eover, with reference to the words of

at "they should always be ruminated

upon so as to be able to gaze on them with ardent application of the soul" (*Collationes In Hexaemeron,* ed. Quaracchi [Florence: Bibliotheca Franciscana Scholastica Medii Aevi, 1934], 218). To meditate, therefore, means to create within us a situation of recollection, of inner silence, in order to reflect upon and assimilate the mysteries of our faith and what God is working within us, and not merely on the things that come and go.

We may undertake this "rumination" in various ways; for example, by taking a brief passage of Sacred Scripture, especially the Gospels, the Acts of the Apostles, or the letters of the apostles, or a passage from a spiritual author that brings us closer and makes the reality of God more present in our day. Or we can even ask our confessor or spiritual director to recommend something to us.

By reading and reflecting on what we have read, dwelling on it, trying to understand what it is saying to me, what it says today, [we are] opening our spirit to what the Lord wants to tell us and teach us. The Holy Rosary is also a prayer of meditation: in repeating the Hail Mary, we are asked to think about and reflect on the mystery that we have just proclaimed. But we can also reflect on some intense spiritual experience, or on words that stayed with us when we were taking part in the Sunday Eucharist. So, you see, there are many ways to meditate and thereby to make contact with

God and to approach God and, in t[...]
on toward heaven.

Dear friends, making time for Go[...]
tal element for spiritual growth. It [...]
who gives us the taste for his myst[...]
ence and action, for feeling how beautiful it is when God
speaks with us; he will enable us to understand more deeply
what he expects of me. This, ultimately, is the very aim of
meditation: to entrust ourselves increasingly to the hands of
God, with trust and love, certain that in the end it is only by
doing his will that we are truly happy.

—General Audience, Castel Gandolfo, August 17, 2011

The Lord Is Present in His Silence

[There is an] important connection between silence and prayer.
Indeed, it is not only our silence that disposes us to listen to
the word of God; in our prayers we often find that we are con-
fronted by God's silence. We feel, as it were, let down; it seems
to us that God neither listens nor responds. Yet God's silence
. . . does not indicate his absence. Christians know well that the
Lord is present and listens, even in the darkness of pain, rejection, and loneliness.

Jesus reassures his disciples and each one of us that God is
well acquainted with our needs at every moment of our life. He
teaches the disciples: "In praying do not heap up empty phrases

Gentiles do; for they think that they will be heard for many words. Do not be like them, for your Father knows what you need before you ask him" (Matthew 6:7-8). An attentive, silent, and open heart is more important than many words. God knows us in our inmost depths, better than we ourselves, and loves us; and knowing this must suffice.

In the Bible, Job's experience is particularly significant in this regard. In a short time, this man loses everything: relatives, possessions, friends, and health. It truly seems that God's attitude toward him is one of abandonment, of total silence. Yet in his relationship with God, Job speaks to God, cries out to God; in his prayers, in spite of all, he keeps his faith intact and, in the end, discovers the value of his experience and of God's silence. And thus, he can finally conclude, addressing the Creator, "I had heard of you by the hearing of the ear, / but now my eye sees you" (Job 42:5). Almost all of us know God only through hearsay, and the more open we are to his silence and to our own silence, the more we truly begin to know him.

This total trust that opens us to the profound encounter with God developed in silence. St. Francis Xavier prayed to the Lord, saying: I do not love You because You can give me paradise or condemn me to hell, but because You are my God. I love You because You are You.

—General Audience, St. Peter's Square, March 7, 2012

JESUS' TEACHING ON PRAYER

This Sunday's Gospel [Luke 11:1-13] presents Jesus to us absorbed in prayer, a little apart from his disciples. When he had finished, one of them said to him, "Lord, teach us to pray" (11:1). Jesus had no objection; he did not speak of strange or esoteric formulas but very simply said, "When you pray, say, 'Father,'" and he taught the Our Father (cf. 11:2-4), taking it from his own prayer in which he himself spoke to God, his Father. St. Luke passes the Our Father on to us in a shorter form than that found in the Gospel according to St. Matthew, which [is the one that] has entered into common usage. We have before us the first words of Sacred Scripture that we learn in childhood. They are impressed in our memory, mold our life, and accompany us to our last breath. They reveal that "we are not ready-made children of God from the start, but that we are meant to become so increasingly by growing more and more deeply in communion with Jesus. Our sonship turns out to be identical with following Christ" (Benedict XVI, *Jesus of Nazareth*, 138).

This prayer also accepts and expresses human material and spiritual needs: "Give us each day our daily bread; and forgive us our sins" (Luke 11:3-4). It is precisely because of the needs and difficulties of every day that Jesus exhorts us forcefully: "I tell you, Ask, and it will be given you; seek, and you will find; knock, and it will be opened to you. For every one who asks receives, and he who seeks finds, and to him who knocks it will be opened" (11:9-10). It is not so much asking in order to satisfy our own desires as rather to keep a lively friendship with

God who, the Gospel continues, will "give the Holy Spirit to those who ask him!" (11:13).

The ancient desert Fathers experienced this, as did contemplatives of all epochs who became, through prayer, friends of God, like Abraham who begged the Lord to spare the few righteous from the destruction of the city of Sodom (cf. Genesis 18:21-32). St. Teresa of Avila addressed . . . her sisters with the words:

> [We must] beseech God to deliver us from these perils for ever and to keep us from all evil! And although our desire for this may not be perfect, let us strive to make the petition. What does it cost us to ask it, since we ask it of One Who is so powerful? (*The Way of Perfection*, trans. E. Allison Peers [Grand Rapids, MI: Christian Classics Ethereal Library, 1964], 166)

Every time we say the Our Father, our voices mingle with the voice of the Church, for those who pray are never alone.

—Angelus Address, Castel Gandolfo, July 25, 2010

A Physical and Spiritual Approach to Prayer

In St. Dominic we can see an example of harmonious integration of contemplation of the divine mysteries and apostolic work. According to the testimonies of people close to him, "he always spoke with God and of God." This observation points to his profound communion with the Lord and, at the same time, to his constant commitment to lead others to this communion with God. He left no writings on prayer, but the Dominican tradition has collected and handed down his living experience in a work called *The Nine Ways of Prayer of St. Dominic.* This book was compiled by a Dominican friar between 1260 and 1288; it helps us to understand something of the saint's interior life and also helps us, with all the different ways, to learn something about how to pray.

There are, then, nine ways to pray, according to St. Dominic, and each one—always before Jesus crucified—expresses a deeply penetrating physical and spiritual approach that fosters recollection and zeal. The first seven ways follow an ascending order, like the steps on a path, toward intimate communion with God, with the Trinity: St. Dominic prayed standing [and] bowed to express humility; lying prostrate on the ground to ask forgiveness for his sins; kneeling in penance to share in the Lord's suffering; [with] his arms wide open; gazing at the crucifix to contemplate supreme Love; and looking heavenwards, feeling drawn to God's world.

Thus, there are three positions—standing, kneeling, lying prostrate on the ground—but with the gaze ever directed to our crucified Lord. However, the last two positions [ways of prayer], on which I would like to reflect briefly, correspond to two of the saint's customary devotional practices.

First, there is personal meditation, in which prayer acquires an even more intimate, fervent, and soothing dimension. After reciting the Liturgy of the Hours and after celebrating Mass, St. Dominic prolonged his conversation with God without setting any time limit. Sitting quietly, he would pause in recollection in an inner attitude of listening while reading a book or gazing at the crucifix. He experienced these moments of closeness to God so intensely that his reactions of joy or of tears were outwardly visible. In this way, through meditation, he absorbed the reality of the faith. Witnesses recounted that at times he entered a kind of ecstasy with his face transfigured, but that immediately afterward, he would humbly resume his daily work, recharged by the power that comes from on high.

Then come his prayers while traveling from one convent to another. He would recite Lauds, Midday Prayer, and Vespers with his companion, and passing through the valleys and across the hills, he would contemplate the beauty of creation. A hymn of praise and thanksgiving to God for his many gifts would well up from his heart, above all for the greatest wonder, the redemptive work of Christ.

Dear friends, St. Dominic reminds us that prayer, personal contact with God, is at the root of the witness to faith that every Christian must bear at home, at work, in social commitments, and even in moments of relaxation. Only this real relationship with God gives us the strength to live through every event with intensity, especially the moments of greatest anguish. This saint also reminds us of the importance of physical positions in our prayer. Kneeling, standing before the Lord, fixing our gaze on the crucifix, silent recollection—these are not of secondary importance but help us to put our whole selves inwardly in touch with God. I would like to recall once again the need, for our spiritual life, to find time every day for quiet prayer; we must make this time for ourselves, to have a little time to talk with God. It will also be a way to help those who are close to us enter into the radiant light of God's presence, which brings the peace and love we all need.

—General Audience, Castel Gandolfo, August 8, 2012

THE WAY OF BEAUTY

I have recalled several times the need for every Christian, in the midst of the many occupations that fill our days, to find time for God and for prayer. The Lord himself gives us many opportunities to remember him. I would like to reflect briefly on one of these channels that can lead to God and can also be of help in our encounter with him. It is the way of artistic expression, part of that *via pulchritudinis*, the "way of beauty," of which I have spoken several times and whose deepest meaning must be recovered by men and women today.

It may have happened on some occasion that you paused before a sculpture, a picture, a few verses of a poem, or a piece of music that you found deeply moving, that gave you a sense of joy, a clear perception, that is, that what you beheld was not only matter—a piece of marble or bronze, a painted canvas, a collection of letters, or an accumulation of sounds—but something greater, something that "speaks," that can touch the heart, communicate a message, uplift the mind.

A work of art is a product of the creative capacity of the human being who in questioning visible reality seeks to discover its deep meaning and to communicate it through the language of forms, color, and sound. Art is able to manifest and make visible the human need to surpass the visible; it expresses the thirst and the quest for the infinite. Indeed, it resembles a door opening on to the infinite, on to a beauty and a truth that go beyond the daily routine. And a work of art can open the eyes of the mind and the heart, impelling us upward.

However, some artistic expressions are real highways to God, the supreme Beauty; indeed, they help us to grow in our relationship with him in prayer. These are works that were born from faith and express faith. We can see an example of this when we visit a Gothic cathedral: we are enraptured by the vertical lines that soar skywards and uplift our gaze and our spirit, while at the same time we feel small yet long for fullness. . . .

Or when we enter a Romanesque church, we are spontaneously prompted to meditate and to pray. We perceive that these splendid buildings contain, as it were, the faith of generations. Or when we listen to a piece of sacred music that plucks at our heartstrings, our mind, as it were, expands and turns naturally to God.

I remember a music concert of Johann Sebastian Bach in Munich conducted by Leonard Bernstein. At the end of the last passage, one of the *Cantatas,* I felt, not by reasoning but in the depths of my heart, that what I had heard had communicated truth to me, the truth of the supreme Composer, and impelled me to thank God. The Lutheran bishop of Munich was next to me, and I said to him spontaneously, "In hearing this, one understands: it is true; such strong faith is true, as well as the beauty that irresistibly expresses the presence of God's truth."

Yet how many pictures or frescoes, fruits of the artist's faith, in their form, in their color, in their light, urge us to think of God and foster within us the desire to draw from the source of all beauty! What Marc Chagall, a great artist, wrote remains profoundly true: that for centuries painters have dipped their paintbrush in that colored alphabet that is the Bible. Thus, how often artistic expression can bring us to remember God, to help us to pray, or even to convert our heart!

Paul Claudel, a famous French poet, playwright, and diplomat, precisely while he was listening in the Cathedral of Notre Dame to the singing of the Magnificat during Christmas Mass in 1886, had a tangible experience of God's presence. He had not entered the church for reasons of faith but rather in order to seek arguments against Christians, and instead, God's grace worked actively in his heart.

Dear friends, I ask you to rediscover the importance of this path also for prayer, for our living relationship with God. Towns and villages throughout the world contain treasures of art that express faith and beckon to us to return to our relationship with God. May the visits to places filled with art, then, not only be opportunities for cultural enrichment—that, too—but may they become, above all, moments of grace, incentives to strengthen our bond and our dialogue with the Lord so that— in switching from simple external reality to the more profound reality it expresses—we may pause to contemplate the ray of beauty that strikes us to the quick, that almost "wounds" us, and that invites us to rise toward God.

I end with a prayer from a psalm, Psalm 27: "One thing have I asked of the LORD , / that will I seek after; / that I may dwell in the house of the LORD / all the days of my life, / to behold the beauty of the LORD, / and to inquire in his temple" (verse 4).

Let us hope that the Lord will help us to contemplate his beauty, both in nature and in works of art, so that we, moved by the light that shines from his, may be a light for our neighbor.

—General Audience, Castel Gandolfo, August 31, 2011

THE WORD OF GOD AND THE LITURGY OF THE HOURS

Among the forms of prayer that emphasize Sacred Scripture, the Liturgy of the Hours has an undoubted place. The Synod Fathers called it "a privileged form of hearing the word of God, inasmuch as it brings the faithful into contact with Scripture and the living Tradition of the Church" (*Propositio* 19). Above all, we should reflect on the profound theological and ecclesial dignity of this prayer.

> In the Liturgy of the Hours, the Church, exercising the priestly office of her Head, offers "incessantly" (1 Thessalonians 5:17) to God the sacrifice of praise, that is, the fruit of lips that confess his name (cf. Hebrews13:15). This prayer is "the voice of a bride speaking to her bridegroom, it is the very prayer that Christ himself, together with his Body, addressed to the Father." (*Principles and Norms for the Liturgy of the Hours*, III, 15)

The Second Vatican Council stated in this regard that

> all who render this service are not only fulfilling a duty of the Church, but also are sharing in the greatest honor of Christ's spouse; for by offering these praises to God they are standing before God's throne in the name of the Church their Mother. (*Sacrosanctum Concilium*, 85).

The Liturgy of the Hours, as the public prayer of the Church, sets forth the Christian ideal of the sanctification of the entire day, marked by the rhythm of hearing the word of God and praying the psalms. In this way every activity can find its point of reference in the praise offered to God. . . .

The Synod asked that this prayer become more widespread among the People of God, particularly the recitation of Morning Prayer and Evening Prayer. This could only lead to greater familiarity with the word of God on the part of the faithful. Emphasis should also be placed on the value of the Liturgy of the Hours for the First Vespers of Sundays and solemnities, particularly in the Eastern Catholic Churches. To this end I recommend that, wherever possible, parishes and religious communities promote this prayer with the participation of the lay faithful.

—Apostolic Exhortation *Verbum Domini*, 62, September 30, 2010

Persisting in Prayer

At times we grow weary of praying; we have the impression that prayer is not so useful for life, that it is not very effective. We are therefore tempted to throw ourselves into activity, to use all the human means for attaining our goals, and we do not turn to God. Jesus himself says that it is necessary to pray always, and does so in a specific parable (cf. Luke 18:1-8).

This parable speaks to us of a judge who does not fear God and is no respecter of persons—a judge without a positive outlook, who only seeks his own interests. He neither fears God's judgment nor respects his neighbor. The other figure is a widow, a person in a situation of weakness. In the Bible the widow and the orphan are in the neediest categories, because they are defenseless and without means. The widow goes to the judge and asks him for justice. Her possibilities of being heard are almost none, because the judge despises her and she can bring no pressure to bear on him. She cannot even appeal to religious principles because the judge does not fear God. Therefore, this widow seems without any recourse. But she insists; she asks tirelessly, importuning him, and in the end she succeeds in obtaining a result from the judge. At this point, Jesus makes a reflection, using the argument *a fortiori:* If a dishonest judge ends by letting himself be convinced by a widow's plea, how much more will God, who is good, answer those who pray to him? God, in fact, is generosity personified; he is merciful and is therefore always disposed to listen to prayers. Therefore, we must never despair but always persist in prayer.

The conclusion of the Gospel passage speaks of faith: "When the Son of man comes, will he find faith on earth?" (Luke 18:8). It is a question that intends to elicit an increase of faith on our part. Indeed, it is clear that prayer must be an expression of faith; otherwise, it is not true prayer. If one does not believe in God's goodness, one cannot pray in a truly appropriate manner. Faith is essential as the basis of a prayerful attitude.

—Homily, St. Peter's Square, October 17, 2010

Lectio Divina: The Prayerful Reading of Sacred Scripture

I would like to review the basic steps of *lectio divina*. It opens with the reading (*lectio*) of a text, which leads to a desire to understand its true content: *What does the biblical text say in itself?* Without this, there is always a risk that the text will become a pretext for never moving beyond our own ideas. Next comes meditation (*meditatio*), which asks: *What does the biblical text say to us?* Here, each person, individually but also as a member of the community, must let himself or herself be moved and challenged. Following this comes prayer (*oratio*), which asks the question: *What do we say to the Lord in response to his word?* Prayer as petition, intercession, thanksgiving, and praise is the primary way by which the word transforms us. Finally, *lectio divina* concludes with contemplation (*contemplatio*), during which we take up, as a gift from God, his own way of seeing and judging reality, and ask ourselves: *What conversion of mind, heart, and life is the Lord asking of us?*

In the Letter to the Romans, St. Paul tells us: "Do not be conformed to this world but be transformed by the renewal of your mind, that you may prove what is the will of God, what is good and acceptable and perfect" (12:2). Contemplation aims at creating within us a truly wise and discerning vision of reality, as God sees it, and at forming within us "the mind of Christ" (1 Corinthians 2:16). The word of God appears here as a criterion for discernment: it is "living and active, sharper than any two-edged sword, piercing to the division of soul and spirit, of joints and marrow, and discerning the thoughts and intentions of the heart" (Hebrews 4:12). We do well also to remember that the process of *lectio divina* is not concluded until it arrives at action (*actio*), which moves the believer to make his or her life a gift for others in charity.

We find the supreme synthesis and fulfillment of this process in the Mother of God. For every member of the faithful, Mary is the model of docile acceptance of God's word, for she "kept all these things, pondering them in her heart" (Luke 2:19; cf. 2:51); she discovered the profound bond which unites, in God's great plan, apparently disparate events, actions, and things.

—Apostolic Exhortation *Verbum Domini*, 87, September 30, 2010

Praying for Christian Unity

As we raise our prayers, we are confident that we will be transformed and brought into conformity with the image of Christ. This is particularly true in the prayer for Christian unity. Indeed, when we implore the gift of the unity of Christ's disciples, we make our own the desire expressed by Jesus Christ on the eve of his passion and death in the prayer he addressed to the Father: "that they may all be one" (John 17:21). The prayer for Christian unity, for this reason, is nothing other than participation in the realization of the divine plan for the Church, and the active commitment to reestablishing unity is a task and a great responsibility for all.

Although in our day we are experiencing the sorrowful situation of division, we Christians can and must look to the future with hope, since Christ's victory means surmounting all that prevents us from sharing the fullness of life with him and with others. The resurrection of Jesus Christ confirms that God's goodness conquers evil and that love conquers death. He accompanies us in the fight against the destructive power of sin that damages humanity and God's entire creation.

The presence of the risen Christ calls all of us Christians to act together in the cause of good. United in Christ, we are called to share his mission, which is to bring hope to wherever injustice, hatred, and desperation prevail. Our divisions dim our witness to Christ. The goal of full unity, which we await in active hope and for which we pray trustingly, is no secondary victory but an important one for the good of the human family.

In the dominant culture today, the idea of victory is often associated with instant success. In the Christian perspective, on the contrary, victory is a long—and in our human eyes—not always uncomplicated process of transformation and growth in goodness. It happens in accordance with God's time, not ours, and requires of us deep faith and patient perseverance. Although the kingdom of God bursts definitively into history with Jesus' resurrection, it has not yet come about fully. The final victory will only be won with the Second Coming of the Lord, which we await with patient hope.

Our expectation of the visible unity of the Church must also be patient and trusting. Only in this frame of mind do our prayers and our daily commitment to Christian unity find their full meaning. The attitude of patient waiting does not mean passivity or resignation but rather a prompt and attentive response to every possibility of communion and brotherhood that the Lord gives us.

—Homily at the Conclusion of the Week of Prayer for Christian Unity, Basilica of St. Paul Outside-the-Walls, January 25, 2012

In Conversation with God

St. Alphonsus Mary Liguori . . . describes prayer as "a necessary and certain means of obtaining salvation, and all the graces that we require for that object" (*The Great Means of Salvation and Perfection,* Introduction). This sentence sums up the way St. Alphonsus understood prayer.

First of all, by saying that it is a means, he reminds us of the goal to be reached. God created us out of love in order to be able to give us life in its fullness; but this goal, this life in fullness, has, as it were, become distant because of sin—we all know it—and only God's grace can make it accessible. To explain this basic truth and to make people understand with immediacy how real the risk of "being lost" is for human beings, St. Alphonsus coined a famous, very elementary maxim that says: "Those who pray will be saved and those who do not will be damned!" Commenting on this lapidary sentence, he added, "In conclusion, to save one's soul without prayer is most difficult, and even (as we have seen) impossible.

. . . But by praying our salvation is made secure, and very easy." And he says further: "If we do not pray, we have no excuse, because the grace of prayer is given to everyone. . . . If we are not saved, the whole fault will be ours; and we shall have our own failure to answer for, because we did not pray" (I, 2, Conclusion).

By saying, then, that prayer is a necessary means, St. Alphonsus wanted us to understand that in no situation of life can we do without prayer, especially in times of trial and difficulty. We must always knock at the door of the Lord confidently, knowing that he cares for all his children, for us. For this reason we are asked not to be afraid to turn to him and to present our requests to him with trust, in the certainty of receiving what we need.

Dear friends, this is the main question: what is really necessary in my life? I answer with St. Alphonsus: "health and all the graces that we need." He means, of course, not only the health of the body, but first of all, that of the soul, which Jesus gives us. More than anything else, we need his liberating presence, which makes us truly fully human and hence fills our existence with joy. And it is only through prayer that we can receive him and his grace, which by enlightening us in every situation, helps us to discern true good; and by strengthening us, it also makes our will effective, that is, renders it capable of doing what we know is good. We often recognize what is good but are unable to do it. With prayer we succeed in doing it. The disciple of the Lord knows he is always exposed to temptation and does not fail to ask God's help in prayer in order to resist it.

St. Alphonsus very interestingly cites the example of St. Philip Neri, who "the very moment when he awoke in the morning, said to God: 'Lord, keep Thy hands over Philip this day; for if not, Philip will betray Thee'" (I, 3, 2). What a great realist! He asks God to keep his hands upon him. We, too, aware of our weakness, must humbly seek God's help, relying on his boundless mercy. St. Alphonsus says in another passage: "We are so poor that we have nothing; but if we pray we are no longer poor. If we are poor, God is rich" (I, 2, 4). And, following in St. Augustine's wake, he invites all Christians not to be afraid to obtain from God, through prayer, the power they do not possess that is necessary in order to do good, in the certainty that the Lord will not refuse his help to whoever prays to him with humility (cf. I, 3, 3).

Dear friends, St. Alphonsus reminds us that the relationship with God is essential in our life. Without the relationship with God, the fundamental relationship is absent. The relationship with God is brought into being in conversation with God, in daily personal prayer, and through participation in the sacraments. This relationship is thus able to grow within us, as can the divine presence that directs us on our way, illuminates it, and makes it safe and peaceful even amidst difficulties and perils.

—General Audience, Castel Gandolfo, August 1, 2012

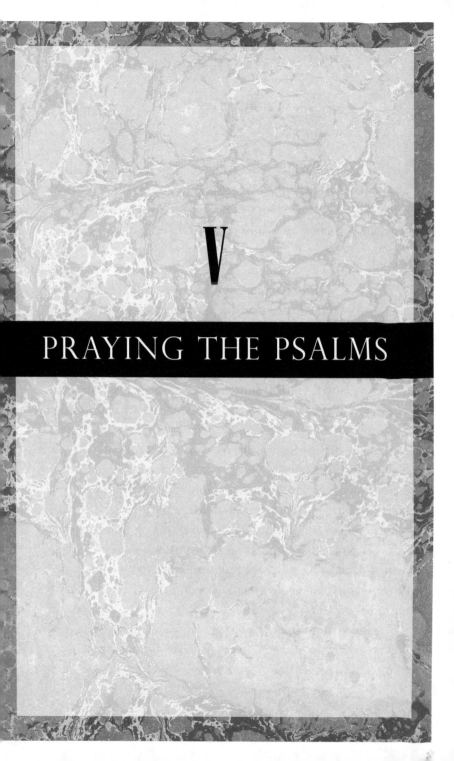

V

PRAYING THE PSALMS

The Psalms Teach Us How to Pray

The Psalter appears as a "formulary" of prayers, a collection of 150 psalms which the biblical tradition offers the people of believers so that they become their and our prayer, our way of speaking and of relating to God. This book expresses the entire human experience with its multiple facets and the whole range of sentiments that accompany human existence.

The psalms express and interweave joy and suffering; the longing for God and the perception of our own unworthiness; happiness and the feeling of abandonment; trust in God and sorrowful loneliness; fullness of life and fear of death. The whole reality of the believer converges in these prayers. The People of Israel first, and then the Church, adopted them as a privileged mediation in relations with the one God and an appropriate response to God's self-revelation in history.

Since the psalms are prayers, they are expressions of the heart and of faith with which everyone can identify and in which that experience of special closeness to God—to which every human being is called—is communicated. Moreover, the whole complexity of human life is distilled in the complexity of the different literary forms of the various psalms: hymns, laments, individual entreaties and collective supplications, hymns of thanksgiving, penitential psalms, sapiential psalms, and the other genres that are to be found in these poetic compositions.

Despite this multiplicity of expression, two great areas that sum up the prayer of the Psalter may be identified: supplication, connected to lamentation, and praise. These are two related dimensions that are almost inseparable, since supplication is motivated by the certainty that God will respond, thus opening a person to praise and thanksgiving, and praise and thanksgiving stem from the experience of salvation received; this implies the need for help, which the supplication expresses.

In his supplication the person praying bewails and describes his situation of anguish, danger, or despair, or, as in the penitential psalms, he confesses his guilt and his sin, asking forgiveness. He discloses his needy state to the Lord, confident that he will be heard, and this involves the recognition of God as good, as desirous of goodness, and as one who "loves the living" (cf. Wisdom 11:26), ready to help, to save, and to forgive. In this way, for example, the psalmist in Psalm 31 prays: "In you, O LORD, I seek refuge; / let me never be put to shame / . . . Take me out of the net which is hidden for me, / for you are my refuge" (31:1, 4). In the lamentation, therefore, something like praise, which is foretold in the hope of divine intervention, can already emerge, and it becomes explicit when divine salvation becomes a reality.

Likewise in the psalms of thanksgiving and praise, recalling the gift received or contemplating the greatness of God's mercy, we also recognize our own smallness and the need to be saved, which is at the root of supplication. In this way we confess to God our condition as creatures, inevitably marked by death yet bearing a radical desire for life. The psalmist therefore exclaims in Psalm 86: "I give thanks to you, O Lord my God, with my whole heart, / and I will glorify your name for ever. / For great is your merciful love toward me; / you have delivered my soul from the depths of Sheol" (86:12-

13). In the prayer of the psalms, supplication and praise are interwoven in this manner and fused in a single hymn that celebrates the eternal grace of the Lord who stoops down to our frailty.

It was precisely in order to permit the people of believers to join in this hymn that the Psalter was given to Israel and to the Church. Indeed, the psalms teach how to pray. In them the word of God becomes a word of prayer—and they are the words of the inspired psalmist—which also becomes the word of the person who prays the psalms.

—General Audience, St. Peter's Square, June 22, 2011

The Psalms, a Language for Our Encounter with God

This is the beauty and the special characteristic of this book of the Bible: the prayers it contains, unlike other prayers we find in Sacred Scripture, are not inserted in a narrative plot that specifies their meaning and role. The psalms are given to the believer exactly as the text of prayers whose sole purpose is to become the prayer of the person who assimilates them and addresses them to God. Since they are a word of God, anyone who prays the psalms speaks to God using the very words that God has given to us, addresses him with the words that he himself has given us. So it is that in praying the psalms, we learn to pray. They are a school of prayer.

Something similar happens when a child begins to speak; namely, he learns how to express his own feelings, emotions, and needs with words that do not belong to him innately but that he learns from his parents and from those who surround him. What the child wishes to express is his own experience, but his means of expression comes from others. Little by little, he makes them his own; the words received from his parents become his words, and through these words, he also learns a way of thinking and feeling; he gains access to a whole world of concepts and in it develops and grows and relates to reality, to people, and to God. In the end his parents' language has become his language; he speaks with words he has received from others but that have now become his own.

This is what happens with the prayer of the psalms. They are given to us so that we may learn to address God, to communicate with him, to speak to him of ourselves with his words, and to find a language for the encounter with God. And through those words, it will also be possible to know and to accept the criteria of his action, to draw closer to the mystery of his thoughts and ways (cf. Isaiah 55:8-9), so as to grow constantly in faith and in love.

Just as our words are not only words but teach us a real and conceptual world, so too these prayers teach us the heart of God, for which reason not only can we speak to God, but we can learn who God is; and in learning how to speak to him, we learn to be a human being, to be ourselves.

In this regard the title which the Jewish tradition has given to the Psalter is significant. It is called *tehillîm,* a Hebrew word that means "praise," from the etymological root that we find in the expression "Alleluia," that is, literally, "Praised be the Lord." This book of prayers, therefore, although it is so multiform and complex with its different literary genres and its structure alternating between praise and supplication, is ultimately a book of praise that teaches us to give thanks, to celebrate the greatness of God's gift, to recognize the beauty of his works, and to glorify his holy name. This is the most appropriate response to the Lord's self-manifestation and to the experience of his goodness.

By teaching us to pray, the psalms teach us that even in desolation, even in sorrow, God's presence endures; it is a source of wonder and of solace. We can weep, implore, intercede, and complain, but in the awareness that we are walking toward the light, where praise can be definitive. As Psalm 36 teaches us, "With you is the fountain of life; / in your light do we see light" (36:9).

—General Audience, St. Peter's Square, June 22, 2011

JESUS' PRAYER ON THE CROSS

What is the meaning of Jesus' prayer, of the cry he addresses to the Father, "My God, my God, why have you forsaken me?" Doubt about his mission, about the Father's presence? Might there not be in this prayer the knowledge that he had been forsaken? The words that Jesus addresses to the Father are the beginning of Psalm 22, in which the psalmist expresses to God his being torn between feeling forsaken and the certain knowledge of God's presence in his people's midst. He, the psalmist, prays: "O my God, I cry by day, but you do not answer; / and by night, but find no rest. / Yet you are holy, enthroned on the praises of Israel" (22:2-3). The psalmist speaks of this "cry" in order to express the full suffering of his prayer to God, seemingly absent: in the moment of anguish, his prayer becomes a cry.

This also happens in our relationship with the Lord: when we face the most difficult and painful situations, when it seems that God does not hear, we must not be afraid to entrust the whole weight of our overburdened hearts to him. We must not fear to cry out to him in our suffering; we must be convinced that God is close, even if he seems silent.

Repeating from the cross the first words of Psalm 22, *"Eli, Eli, lama sabachthani?"*—"My God, my God, why have you forsaken me?" (Matthew 27:46), uttering the words of the psalm, Jesus prays at the moment of his ultimate rejection by men, at the moment of abandonment; yet he prays, with the psalm, in the awareness of God's presence, even in that hour when he is feeling the human drama of death.

However, a question arises within us: how is it possible that such a powerful God does not intervene to save his Son from this terrible trial? It is important to understand that Jesus' prayer is not the cry of one who meets death with despair, nor is it the cry of one who knows he has been forsaken. At this moment, Jesus makes his own the whole of Psalm 22, the psalm of the suffering People of Israel. In this way he takes upon himself not only the sin of his people but also that of all men and women who are suffering from the oppression of evil, and at the same time, he places all this before God's own heart, in the certainty that his cry will be heard in the resurrection: "The cry of extreme anguish is at the same time the certainty of an answer from God, the certainty of salvation—not only for Jesus himself, but for 'many'" (Benedict XVI, *Jesus of Nazareth: Part Two*, 213–214).

In this prayer of Jesus are contained his extreme trust and his abandonment into God's hands, even when God seems absent, even when he seems to be silent, complying with a plan incomprehensible to us. In the *Catechism of the Catholic Church*, we read: "In the redeeming love that always united him to the Father, he assumed us in the state of our waywardness of sin, to the point that he could say in our name from the cross: 'My God, my God, why have you forsaken me?'" (603). He is suffering in communion with us and for us, which derives from love and already bears within it redemption, the victory of love.

The bystanders at the foot of the cross of Jesus fail to understand, thinking that his cry is a supplication addressed to Elijah. In the scene they seek to assuage his thirst in order to prolong his life and to find out whether Elijah will truly come to his aid, but with a loud cry, Jesus' earthly life comes to an end, as well as their wish.

At the supreme moment, Jesus gives vent to his heart's grief but, at the same time, makes clear the meaning of the Father's presence and his consent to the Father's plan of the salvation of humanity.

We, too, have to face ever anew the "today" of suffering of God's silence—we express it so often in our prayers—but we also find ourselves facing the "today" of the resurrection, of the response of God, who took upon himself our sufferings to carry them together with us and to give us the firm hope that they will be overcome (cf. Encyclical *Spe Salvi*, 35–40).

Dear friends, let us lay our daily crosses before God in our prayers, in the certainty that he is present and hears us. Jesus' cry reminds us that in prayer we must surmount the barriers of our "ego" and our problems and open ourselves to the needs and suffering of others.

May the prayer of Jesus dying on the cross teach us to pray lovingly for our many brothers and sisters who are oppressed by the weight of daily life, who are living through difficult moments, who are in pain, who have no word of comfort; let us place all this before God's heart, so that they, too, may feel the love of God who never abandons us.

—General Audience, Paul VI Audience Hall, February 8, 2012

His Mercy Endures Forever!

This psalm [136] was called the "Great Hallel," that is, the grandiose and solemn praise that the Jews intoned during their Passover liturgy. . . . Let us first reflect on the refrain "for his mercy endures for ever." At the center of the phrase, the word "mercy" rings out. In fact, it is a legitimate but limited translation of the original Hebrew term *hesed*. This is actually a word that belongs to the characteristic terminology used in the Bible to express the covenant that exists between the Lord and his people. The term seeks to define the attitudes deriving from this relationship: faithfulness, loyalty, love, and, of course, God's mercy.

We have here a concise summary that portrays the deep personal bond established by the Creator with his creature. In this relationship, God does not appear in the Bible as an impassive and implacable Lord against whose mysterious power it is useless to struggle. Instead, he shows himself as a person who loves his creatures, watches over them, follows them on their way through history, and suffers because of the infidelities with which the people often oppose his *hesed*, his merciful and fatherly love.

The first visible sign of this divine love, says the psalmist, is to be sought in creation and then in history. The gaze, full of admiration and wonder, will rest first of all on creation: the skies, the earth, the seas, the sun, the moon, and the stars. Even before discovering the God who reveals himself in the history of a people, there is a cosmic revelation, open to all, offered to the whole of humanity by the one Creator, "God of gods" and "Lord of lords" (Psalm 136:2, 3).

As sung in Psalm 19: "The heavens are telling the glory of God; / and the firmament proclaims his handiwork. / Day to day pours forth speech, / and night to night declares knowledge" (19:1-2). Thus, a divine message exists, secretly engraved in creation and a sign of the *hesed*, the loving fidelity of God who gives his creatures being and life, water and food, light and time.

A clear vision is essential in order to contemplate this divine revelation, recalling the recommendation of the Book of Wisdom that invites us to recognize "from the greatness and beauty of created things / comes a corresponding perception of their Creator" (Wisdom 13:5; cf. Romans 1:20).

Prayerful praise, therefore, flows from contemplation of the "marvelous works" (cf. Psalm 136:4) that God has wrought in creation that are transformed into a joyful hymn of praise and thanksgiving to the Lord.

—General Audience, St. Peter's Square, November 9, 2005

The Lord, Our Shepherd, Walks with Us

Turning to the Lord in prayer implies a radical act of trust, in the awareness that one is entrusting oneself to God who is good, "merciful and gracious, slow to anger, and abounding in steadfast love and faithfulness" (Exodus 34:6-7; Psalm 86:15; cf. Joel 2:13; Jonah 4:2; Psalm 103:8; 145:8; Nehemiah 9:17). For this reason I would like to reflect with you today on a psalm that is totally imbued with trust, in which the psalmist expresses his serene certainty that he is guided and protected, safe from every danger, because the Lord is his shepherd. It is Psalm 23 [22, according to the Greco-Latin numbering], a text familiar to all and loved by all.

"The Lord is my shepherd, I shall not want" (Psalm 23:1): the beautiful prayer begins with these words, evoking the nomadic environment of sheep farming and the experience of familiarity between the shepherd and the sheep that make up his little flock. The image calls to mind an atmosphere of trust, intimacy, and tenderness: the shepherd knows each one of his sheep and calls them by name, and they follow him because they recognize him and trust in him (cf. John 10:2-4).

He tends them, looks after them as precious possessions, ready to defend them, to guarantee their well-being and enable them to live a peaceful life. They can lack nothing as long as the shepherd is with them. The psalmist refers to this experience by calling God his shepherd and letting God lead him to safe pastures: "He makes me lie down in green pastures. / He leads me beside still waters; / he restores my soul. / He leads me in paths of righteousness / for his name's sake" (Psalm 23:2-3).

The vision that unfolds before our eyes is that of green pastures and springs of clear water, oases of peace to which the shepherd leads his flock, symbols of the places of life toward which the Lord leads the psalmist, who feels like the sheep lying on the grass beside a stream, resting rather than in a state of tension or alarm, peaceful and trusting, because it is a safe place; the water is fresh and the shepherd is watching over them.

And let us not forget here that the scene elicited by the psalm is set in a land that is largely desert, on which the scorching sun beats down, where the Middle Eastern semi-nomadic shepherd lives with his flock in the parched steppes that surround the villages. Nevertheless, the shepherd knows where to find grass and fresh water, essential to life; he can lead the way to oases in which the soul is "restored" and where it is possible to recover strength and new energy to start out afresh on the journey.

As the psalmist says, God guides him to "green pastures" and "still waters," where everything is superabundant, everything is given in plenty. If the Lord is the shepherd even in the desert, a desolate place of death, the certainty of a radical presence of life is not absent so that he is able to say, "I shall not want." Indeed, the shepherd has at heart the good of his flock; he adapts his own pace and needs to those of his sheep; he walks and lives with them, leading them on paths "of righteousness," that is, suitable for them, paying attention to their needs and not to his own. The safety of his sheep is a priority for him, and he complies with this in leading his flock.

Dear brothers and sisters, if we follow the "Good Shepherd"—no matter how difficult, tortuous, or long the pathways of our life may seem, even through spiritual deserts without water and under the scorching sun of rationalism— with the guidance of Christ the Good Shepherd, we, too, like the psalmist, may be sure that we are walking on "paths of righteousness" and that the Lord is leading us, is ever close to us, and that we "shall lack nothing."

—General Audience, St. Peter's Square, October 5, 2011

Following the Shepherd Leads to God's House

"You prepare a table before me / in the presence of my enemies; / you anoint my head with oil, / my cup overflows" (Psalm 23:5).

The Lord is now presented as the One who welcomes the person praying with signs of generous hospitality, full of attention. The divine host lays the food on the "table," a term that in Hebrew means, in its primitive sense, the animal skin that was spread out on the ground and on which the food for the common meal was set out. It is a gesture of sharing, not only of food, but also of life, in an offering of communion and friendship that creates bonds and expresses solidarity. Then there is the munificent gift of scented oil poured on the head, which with its fragrance brings relief from the scorching of the desert sun, refreshes and calms the skin, and gladdens the spirit.

Lastly, the cup overflowing with its exquisite wine, shared with superabundant generosity, adds a note of festivity. Food, oil, and wine are gifts that bring life and give joy, because they go beyond what is strictly necessary and express the free giving and abundance of love. Psalm 104 proclaims:

> You cause the grass to grow for the cattle,
>   and plants for man to cultivate,
> that he may bring forth food from the earth,
>   and wine to gladden the heart of man,
> oil to make his face shine,
>   and bread to strengthen man's heart. (verses 14-15)

The psalmist becomes the object of much attention, for which reason he sees himself as a wayfarer who finds shelter in a hospitable tent, whereas his enemies have to stop and watch, unable to intervene, since the one whom they considered their prey has been led to safety and has become a sacred guest who cannot be touched. And the psalmist is us, if we truly are believers in communion with Christ. When God opens his tent to us to receive us, nothing can harm us. Then when the traveler sets out afresh, the divine protection is extended and accompanies him on his journey: "Surely goodness and mercy shall follow me / all the days of my life; / and I shall dwell in the house of the LORD for ever" (Psalm 23:6).

The goodness and faithfulness of God continue to escort the psalmist, who comes out of the tent and resumes his journey. But it is a journey that acquires new meaning and becomes a pilgrimage to the Temple of the Lord, the holy place in which the praying person wants to "dwell" forever and to which he also wants to "return." The Hebrew verb used here has the meaning of "to return," but with a small vowel change can be understood as "to dwell." Moreover, this is how it is rendered by the ancient versions and by the majority of the modern translations. Both meanings may be retained: to return and dwell in the Temple, as every Israelite desires, and to dwell near God, close to him and to goodness.

This is what every believer yearns and longs for: truly to be able to live where God is, close to him. Following the Shepherd leads to God's house; this is the destination of every journey, the longed-for oasis in the desert, the tent of shelter in escaping from enemies, a place of peace where God's kindness and faithful love may be felt, day after day, in the serene joy of time without end.

—General Audience, St. Peter's Square, October 5, 2011

Praying the Psalms in Christ and with Christ

The Jewish tradition has given many psalms specific names, attributing most of them to King David. A figure of outstanding human and theological depth, David was a complex figure who went through the most varied fundamental experiences of life. When he was young, he was a shepherd of his father's flock; then passing through chequered and at times dramatic vicissitudes, he became king of Israel and pastor of the People of God. A man of peace, he fought many wars. Unflagging and tenacious in his quest for God, he betrayed God's love, and this is characteristic: he always remained a seeker of God even though he sinned frequently and seriously. As a humble penitent, he received the divine pardon, accepted the divine punishment, and accepted a destiny marked by suffering. Thus, David with all his weaknesses was a king "after the heart of God" (cf. 1 Samuel 13:14), that is, a passionate man of prayer, a man who knew what it meant to implore and to praise. The connection of the psalms with this outstanding king of Israel is therefore important because he is a messianic figure, an anointed one of the Lord, in whom, in a certain way, the mystery of Christ is foreshadowed.

Equally important and meaningful are the manner and frequency with which the words of the psalms are taken up in the New Testament, assuming and accentuating the prophetic value suggested by the connection of the Psalter with the messianic figure of David. In the Lord Jesus, who in his earthly life prayed the psalms, they were definitively fulfilled and revealed their fullest and most profound meaning.

The prayers of the Psalter with which we speak to God speak to us of him; they speak to us of the Son, an "image of the invisible God" (Colossians 1:15), which fully reveals to us the Father's face. Christians, therefore, in praying the psalms, pray to the Father in Christ and with Christ, assuming those hymns in a new perspective, which has in the paschal mystery the ultimate key to its interpretation. The horizon of the person praying thus opens to unexpected realities; every psalm acquires a new light in Christ, and the Psalter can shine out in its full, infinite richness.

Dear brothers and sisters, let us therefore take this holy book in our hands; let us allow God to teach us to turn to him; let us make the Psalter a guide which helps and accompanies us daily on the path of prayer. And let us too ask, as did Jesus' disciples, "Lord, teach us to pray" (Luke 11:1), opening our hearts to receive the Teacher's prayer, in which all prayers are brought to completion. Thus, made sons in the Son, we shall be able to speak to God, calling him "Our Father."

—General Audience, St. Peter's Square, June 22, 2011

Oh, How I Love Your Law!

In today's catechesis I would like to reflect on Psalm 119. It is a very special psalm, unique of its kind. This is first of all because of its length. Indeed, it is composed of 176 verses divided into twenty-two stanzas of eight verses each. Moreover, its special feature is that it is an "acrostic in alphabetical order"; in other words, it is structured in accordance with the Hebrew alphabet that consists of twenty-two letters. Each stanza begins with a letter of this alphabet, and the first letter of the first word of each of the eight verses in the stanza begins with this letter. This is both original and indeed a demanding literary genre in which the author of the psalm must have had to summon up all his skill.

However, what is most important for us is this psalm's central theme. In fact, it is an impressive, solemn canticle on the *Torah* of the Lord, that is, on his law, a term which in its broadest and most comprehensive meaning should be understood as a teaching, an instruction, a rule of life. The *Torah* is a revelation; it is a word of God that challenges the human being and elicits his response of trusting obedience and generous love.

This psalm is steeped in love for the word of God, whose beauty, saving power, and capacity for giving joy and life it celebrates, because the divine law is not a heavy yoke of slavery but a liberating gift of grace that brings happiness. "I will delight in your statutes; / I will not forget your word," the psalmist declares (Psalm 119:16), and then, "Lead me in the path of your commandments, / for I delight in it" (119:35). And further: "Oh, how I love your law! / It is my meditation all the day" (119:97).

The law of the Lord, his word, is the center of the praying person's life; he finds comfort in it, he makes it the subject of meditation, he treasures it in his heart: "I have laid up your word in my heart, / that I might not sin against you" (Psalm 119:11), and this is the secret of the psalmist's happiness; and then, again, "The godless besmear me with lies, / but with my whole heart I keep your precepts" (119:69).

The psalmist's faithfulness stems from listening to the word, from pondering it in his inmost self, meditating on it and cherishing it, just as did Mary, who "kept all these things, pondering them in her heart" (Luke 2:19). . . . And if the first verses of our psalm begin by proclaiming "blessed" those "who walk in the law of the LORD" (Psalm 119:1b) and "who keep his testimonies" (119:2a), it is once again the Virgin Mary who brings to completion the perfect figure of the believer described by the psalmist. It is she, in fact, who is the true "blessed," proclaimed such by Elizabeth because "she . . . believed that there would be a fulfillment of what was spoken to her from the Lord" (Luke 1:45). Moreover, it was to her and to her faith that Jesus himself bore witness when he answered the woman who had cried, "Blessed is the womb that bore you" with "Blessed rather are those who hear the word of God and keep it!" (11:27-28). Of course, Mary is blessed because she carried the Savior in her womb, but especially because she accepted God's announcement and because she was an attentive and loving custodian of his word.

Psalm 119 is thus woven around this word of life and blessedness. If its central theme is the "word" and "law" of the Lord, next to these terms in almost all the verses such synonyms recur as "precepts," "statutes," "commandments," "ordinances," "promises," and "judgment"; and then so many verbs relating to them, such as "observe," "keep," "understand," "learn," "love," "meditate," and "live."

The entire alphabet unfolds through the twenty-two stanzas of this psalm and also the whole of the vocabulary of the believer's trusting relationship with God; we find in it praise, thanksgiving, and trust, but also supplication and lamentation. However, they are always imbued with the certainty of divine grace and of the power of the word of God. Even the verses more heavily marked by grief and by a sense of darkness remain open to hope and are permeated by faith.

"My soul cleaves to the dust; / revive me according to your word" (Psalm 119:25), the psalmist trustingly prays. "I have become like a wineskin in the smoke, / yet I have not forgotten your statutes" (119:83) is his cry as a believer. His fidelity, even when it is put to the test, finds strength in the Lord's word: "Then shall I have an answer for those who taunt me, / for I trust in your word" (119:42), he says firmly. And even when he faces the anguishing prospect of death, the Lord's commandments are his reference point and his hope of victory: "They have almost made an end of me on earth; / but I have not forsaken your precepts" (119:87).

The law of the Lord, the object of the passionate love of the psalmist as well as of every believer, is a source of life. The desire to understand it, to observe it, and to direct the whole of one's being by it is characteristic of every righteous person who is faithful to the Lord and who "on his law . . . meditates day and night," as Psalm 1 recites (1:2). The law of God is a way to be kept "in the heart," as the well-known text of the *Shema* in Deuteronomy says:

> "Hear, O Israel: . . . And these words which I command you this day shall be upon your heart; and you shall teach them diligently to your children, and shall talk of them when you sit in your house, and when you walk by the way, and when you lie down, and when you rise." (6:4, 6-7)

The law of God, at the center of life, demands that the heart listen. It is a listening that does not consist of servile but rather of filial, trusting, and conscious obedience. Listening to the word is a personal encounter with the Lord of life, an encounter that must be expressed in concrete decisions and become a journey and a *sequela*. When Jesus is asked what one should do to inherit eternal life, he points to the way of observance of the law but indicates what should be done to bring it to completion: "You lack one thing; go, sell what you have, and give to the poor, and you will have treasure in heaven; and come, follow me!" (Mark 10:21ff.). Fulfillment of the law is following Jesus, traveling on the road that Jesus took, in the company of Jesus.

—General Audience, St. Peter's Square, November 9, 2011

THE LORD IS MY PORTION

There is a verse in Psalm 119 on which I would now like to reflect. It is verse 57: "The LORD is my portion; / I promise to keep your words." In other psalms, too, the person praying affirms that the Lord is his "portion," his inheritance: "The LORD is my chosen portion and my cup," Psalm 16 (verse 5) says. "God is the strength of my heart and my portion for ever" is the protestation of faith of the faithful person in Psalm 73 (verse 26b), and again, in Psalm 142, the psalmist cries to the Lord, "You are my refuge, / my portion in the land of the living" (verse 5b).

This term "portion" calls to mind the event of the division of the Promised Land between the tribes of Israel, when no piece of land was assigned to the Levites because their "portion" was the Lord himself. Two texts of the Pentateuch, using the term in question, are explicit in this regard. The Lord said to Aaron, "You shall have no inheritance in their land, neither shall you have any portion among them; I am your *portion* and your inheritance among the People of Israel," as the Book of Numbers (18:20, emphasis added) declares and as Deuteronomy reaffirms: "Therefore Levi has no *portion* or inheritance with his brothers; the LORD is his inheritance, as the LORD your God said to him" (10:9, emphasis added; cf. Deuteronomy 18:2; Joshua 13:33; Ezekiel 44:28).

The priests, who belong to the tribe of Levi, cannot be landowners in the land that God was to bequeath as a legacy to his people, thus bringing to completion the promise he had made to Abraham (cf. Genesis 12:1-7). The ownership of land, a fundamental element for permanence and for survival, was a sign of blessing because it presupposed the possibility of building a house, of raising children, of cultivating the fields, and of living on the produce of the earth.

Well, the Levites, mediators of the sacred and of the divine blessing, unlike the other Israelites, could not own possessions, this external sign of blessing and source of subsistence. Totally dedicated to the Lord, they had to live on him alone, reliant on his provident love and on the generosity of their brethren, without any other inheritance, since God was their portion. God was the land that enabled them to live to the full.

The person praying in Psalm 119 then applies this reality to himself: "The LORD is my portion." His love for God and for his word leads him to make the radical decision to have the Lord as his one possession and also to treasure his words as a precious gift more valuable than any legacy or earthly possession. There are two different ways in which our verse may be translated, and it could also be translated as "my portion LORD, as I have said, is to preserve your words." The two translations are not contradictory but, on the contrary, complete each other: the psalmist meant that his portion was the Lord but that preserving the divine words was also part of his inheritance, as he was to say later in verse 111: "Your testimonies are my heritage for ever; / yes, they are the joy of my heart." This is the happiness of the psalmist; like the Levites, he has been given the word of God as his portion, his inheritance.

Dear brothers and sisters, these verses are also of great importance for all of us. First of all, they are important for priests, who are called to live on the Lord and his word alone with no other means of security, with him as their one possession and as their only source of true life. In this light, one understands the free choice of celibacy for the kingdom of heaven in order to rediscover it in its beauty and power.

Yet these verses are also important for all the faithful, the People of God that belong to him alone, "a kingdom and priests" for the Lord (cf. 1 Peter 2:9; Revelation 1:6, 5:10) called to the radicalism of the gospel, witnesses of the life brought by Christ, the new and definitive "High Priest" who gave himself as a sacrifice for the salvation of the world (cf. Hebrews 2:17; 4:14-16; 5:5-10; 9:11ff.). The Lord and his word: these are our "land," in which to live in communion and in joy.

Let us therefore permit the Lord to instill this love for his word in our hearts and to grant that we may always place him and his holy will at the center of our life. Let us ask that our prayers and the whole of our life be illuminated by the word of God, the lamp to light our footsteps and a light on our path, as Psalm 119 (cf. verse 105) says, so that we may walk safely in the land of men. And may Mary, who generously welcomed the Word, be our guide and comfort, the polestar that indicates the way to happiness.

Then we, too, shall be able to rejoice in our prayers, like the praying person of Psalm 16, in the unexpected gifts of the Lord and in the undeserved legacy that has fallen to us: "The LORD is my chosen portion and my cup; . . . / The lines have fallen for me in pleasant places; / yea, I have a goodly heritage" (Psalm 16:5, 6).

—General Audience, St. Peter's Square, November 5, 2011

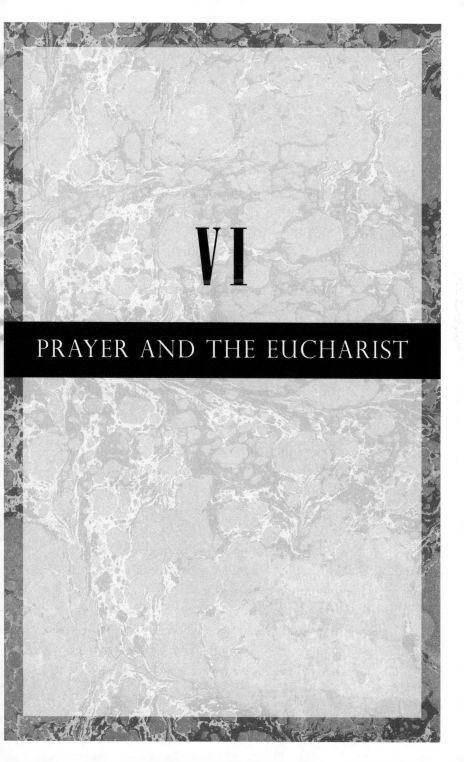

VI

PRAYER AND THE EUCHARIST

THE GIFT OF COMMUNION

The idea of communion as participation in Trinitarian life is illuminated with special intensity in John's Gospel.

Here, the communion of love that binds the Son to the Father and to men and women is at the same time the model and source of the fraternal communion that must unite disciples with one another: "Love one another as I have loved you" (John 15:12; cf. 13:34); "That they may all be one . . . even as we are one" (17:21-22). Hence, it is communion of men and women with the Trinitarian God and communion of men and women with one another.

During the time of his earthly pilgrimage, the disciple can already share through communion with the Son in his divine life and that of the Father: "Our fellowship is with the Father and with his Son Jesus Christ" (1 John 1:3).

This life of fellowship with God and with one another is the proper goal of gospel proclamation, the goal of conversion to Christianity: "That which we have seen and heard we proclaim also to you, so that you may have fellowship with us" (1 John 1:3).

Thus, this twofold communion with God and with one another is inseparable. Wherever communion with God—which is communion with the Father, the Son, and the Holy Spirit—is destroyed, the root and source of our communion with one another is destroyed. And wherever we do not live communion among ourselves, communion with the Trinitarian God is not alive and true either, as we have heard.

Let us now go a step further. Communion, a fruit of the Holy Spirit, is nourished by the Eucharistic Bread (cf. 1 Corinthians 10:16-17) and is expressed in fraternal relations in a sort of anticipation of the future world.

In the Eucharist, Jesus nourishes us; he unites us with himself, with his Father, with the Holy Spirit, and with one another. This network of unity that embraces the world is an anticipation of the future world in our time.

Precisely in this way, since it is an anticipation of the future world, communion is also a gift with very real consequences. It lifts us from our loneliness, from being closed in on ourselves, and makes us sharers in the love that unites us to God and to one another.

It is easy to understand how great this gift is if we only think of the fragmentation and conflicts that afflict relations between individuals, groups, and entire peoples. And if the gift of unity in the Holy Spirit does not exist, the fragmentation of humanity is inevitable.

"Communion" is truly the good news, the remedy given to us by the Lord to fight the loneliness that threatens everyone today, the precious gift that makes us feel welcomed and beloved by God, in the unity of his People gathered in the name of the Trinity. It is the light that makes the Church shine forth like a beacon raised among the peoples.

"If we say we have fellowship with him while we walk in darkness, we lie and do not live according to the truth; but if we walk in the light, as he is in the light, we have fellowship with one another" (1 John 1:6ff.).

Thus, the Church, despite all the human frailties that mark her historical profile, is revealed as a marvelous creation of love, brought into being to bring Christ close to every man and every woman who truly desire to meet him, until the end of time. And in the Church, the Lord always remains our contemporary. Scripture is not something of the past. The Lord does not speak in the past but speaks in the present; he speaks to us today, he enlightens us, he shows us the way through life, he gives us communion, and thus he prepares us and opens us to peace.

—General Audience, St. Peter's Square, March 29, 2006

Christ, the Bread of Life, Feeds Us

Chapter six of John's Gospel [6:1-14] . . . opens with the scene of the multiplication of the loaves, which Jesus later comments on in the synagogue of Capernaum, pointing to himself as the "bread" that gives life. Jesus' actions are on par with those of the Last Supper. He "took the loaves, and when he had given thanks, he distributed them to those who were seated," the Gospel says (John 6:11). The insistence on the topic of "bread," which is shared, and on thanksgiving (6:11, in Greek, *eucharistesas*) recalls the Eucharist, Christ's sacrifice for the world's salvation.

The Evangelist observes that the feast of the Passover is already at hand (cf. John 6:4). His gaze is turned to the cross, the gift of love, and to the Eucharist, the perpetuation of this gift: Christ makes himself the Bread of life for humankind. St. Augustine comments:

> Who is the Bread of heaven, but Christ? But in order that man might eat Angels' Bread, the Lord of Angels was made Man. For if He had not been made Man, we should not have His Flesh; if we had not His Flesh, we should not eat the Bread of the Altar. (*Sermon* 130, 2)

The Eucharist is the human being's ongoing, important encounter with God in which the Lord makes himself our food and gives himself to transform us into him.

A boy's presence is also mentioned in the scene of the multiplication. On perceiving the problem of feeding so many hungry people, he shared the little he had brought with him: five loaves and two fish (cf. John 6:9). The miracle was not worked from nothing, but from a first modest sharing of what a simple lad had brought with him. Jesus does not ask us for what we do not have. Rather, he makes us see that if each person offers the little he has, the miracle can always be repeated: God is capable of multiplying our small acts of love and making us share in his gift.

The crowd was impressed by the miracle: it sees in Jesus the new Moses, worthy of power, and in the new manna, the future guaranteed. However, the people stopped at the material element, which they had eaten, and the Lord, "perceiving then that they were about to come and take him by force to make him king, . . . withdrew again to the hills by himself" (John 6:15). Jesus is not an earthly king who exercises dominion but a king who serves, who stoops down to human beings, not only to satisfy their physical hunger, but above all their deeper hunger, the hunger for guidance, meaning, and truth, the hunger for God.

Dear brothers and sisters, let us ask the Lord to enable us to rediscover the importance of feeding ourselves not only on bread but also on truth, on love, on Christ, on Christ's Body, taking part faithfully and with profound awareness in the Eucharist so as to be ever more closely united with him. Indeed, "it is not the Eucharistic food that is changed into us, but rather we who are mysteriously transformed by it. Christ nourishes us by uniting us to himself" (Apostolic Exhortation *Sacramentum Caritatis*, 70).

—Angelus Address, Castel Gandolfo, July 29, 2012

WE CAN'T LIVE WITHOUT THE EUCHARIST

Dear brothers and sisters, the Eucharist is at the root of every form of holiness, and each of us is called to the fullness of life in the Holy Spirit. . . . This most holy mystery thus needs to be firmly believed, devoutly celebrated, and intensely lived in the Church. Jesus' gift of himself in the sacrament that is the memorial of his passion tells us that the success of our lives is found in our participation in the Trinitarian life offered to us truly and definitively in him. The celebration and worship of the Eucharist enable us to draw near to God's love and to persevere in that love until we are united with the Lord whom we love. The offering of our lives, our fellowship with the whole community of believers, and our solidarity with all men and women are essential aspects of that *logiké latreía,* spiritual worship, holy and pleasing to God (cf. Romans 12:1), which transforms every aspect of our human existence, to the glory of God.

I therefore ask all pastors to spare no effort in promoting an authentically Eucharistic Christian spirituality. Priests, deacons, and all those who carry out a Eucharistic ministry should always be able to find in this service, exercised with care and constant preparation, the strength and inspiration needed for their personal and communal path of sanctification. I exhort the lay faithful, and families in particular, to find ever anew in the sacrament of Christ's love the energy needed to make their lives an authentic sign of the presence of the risen Lord. I ask all consecrated men and women to show by their Eucharistic lives the splendor and the beauty of belonging totally to the Lord.

At the beginning of the fourth century, Christian worship was still forbidden by the imperial authorities. Some Christians in North Africa, who felt bound to celebrate the Lord's Day, defied the prohibition. They were martyred after declaring that it was not possible for them to live without the Eucharist, the food of the Lord: *sine dominico non possumus* [without Sunday we cannot]. May these martyrs of Abitinae, in union with all those saints and those beatified who made the Eucharist the center of their lives, intercede for us and teach us to be faithful to our encounter with the risen Christ. We, too, cannot live without partaking of the sacrament of our salvation; we, too, desire to be *iuxta dominicam viventes* [living according to Sunday], to reflect in our lives what we celebrate on the

Lord's Day. That day is the day of our definitive deliverance. Is it surprising, then, that we should wish to live every day in that newness of life that Christ has brought us in the mystery of the Eucharist?

—Apostolic Exhortation *Sacramentum Caritatis*, 94–95,
February 22, 2007

GOD FREELY GIVES HIMSELF TO US

At the Last Supper, Jesus summed up the whole of his life in an act that is inscribed in the great paschal blessing to God, an act that he lives as Son in thanksgiving to the Father for his immense love. Jesus broke the bread and shared it, but with a new depth, because he was giving himself. He took the cup and shared it so that all might drink from it, but with this gesture he was giving the "new covenant of his blood" [cf. Luke 22:20]—he was giving himself.

Jesus anticipated the act of supreme love, obedience to the Father's will: the sacrifice of the cross. His life will be taken on the cross, but he was already offering it himself. So it is that Christ's death is not reduced to a violent execution but was transformed by him into a free act of love, of self-giving, which passed through death itself victoriously and reaffirmed the goodness of creation that came from God's hands, that was humiliated by sin and redeemed at last. This immense gift is accessible to us in the Sacrament of the Eucharist. God gives himself to us—to open our life to him, to involve it in the mystery of love of the cross, to make it share in the eternal mystery from which we come, and to anticipate the new condition of full life in God, of which we live in expectation.

—Homily, 25th Italian National Eucharistic Congress, Ancona, September 11, 2011

Entering into the Very Life of Jesus

Everything begins, one might say, from the heart of Christ, who at the Last Supper, on the eve of his passion, thanked and praised God and, by so doing, with the power of his love transformed the meaning of death, which he was on his way to encounter. The fact that the Sacrament of the Altar acquired the name "Eucharist"—"thanksgiving"—expresses precisely this: that changing the substance of the bread and wine into the Body and Blood of Christ is the fruit of the gift that Christ made of himself, the gift of a love stronger than death, divine love that raised him from the dead. This is why the Eucharist is the food of eternal life, the Bread of life. From Christ's heart, from his "Eucharistic prayer" on the eve of his passion, flows that dynamism that transforms reality in its cosmic, human, and historical dimensions. All things proceed from God, from the omnipotence of his Triune love, incarnate in Jesus. Christ's heart is steeped in this love; therefore he can thank and praise God even in the face of betrayal and violence, and in this way, he changes things, people, and the world.

This transformation is possible thanks to a communion stronger than division, the communion of God himself. The word "communion," which we also use to designate the Eucharist, in itself sums up the vertical and horizontal dimensions of Christ's gift.

The words "to receive communion," referring to the act of eating the Bread of the Eucharist, are beautiful and very eloquent. In fact, when we do this act, we enter into communion with the very life of Jesus, into the dynamism of this life, which is given to us and for us. From God, through Jesus, to us, a unique communion is transmitted through the Blessed Eucharist.

—Homily, Solemnity of Corpus Christi, Basilica of St. John Lateran, June 23, 2011

Do We Desire to Receive Jesus?

"I have earnestly desired to eat this Passover with you before I suffer" (Luke 22:15). With these words, Jesus began the celebration of his final meal and the institution of the Holy Eucharist. Jesus approached that hour with eager desire. In his heart he awaited the moment when he would give himself to his own under the appearance of bread and wine. He awaited that moment, which would in some sense be the true messianic wedding feast: when he would transform the gifts of this world and become one with his own, so as to transform them and thus inaugurate the transformation of the world. In this eager desire of Jesus, we can recognize the desire of God himself—his expectant love for mankind, for his creation. A love that awaits the moment of union, a love that wants to draw mankind to itself and thereby fulfill the desire of all creation, for creation eagerly awaits the revelation of the children of God (cf. Romans 8:19). Jesus desires us, he awaits us.

But what about ourselves? Do we really desire him? Are we anxious to meet him? Do we desire to encounter him, to become one with him, to receive the gifts he offers us in the Holy Eucharist? Or are we indifferent, distracted, busy with other things? From Jesus' banquet parables, we realize that he knows all about empty places at the table, invitations refused, lack of interest in him and his closeness. For us, the empty places at the table of the Lord's wedding feast, whether excusable or not, are no longer a parable but a reality in those very countries to which he had revealed his closeness in a special way. Jesus also knew about guests who come to the banquet without being robed in the wedding garment—they come not to rejoice in his presence but merely out of habit, since their hearts are elsewhere.

In one of his homilies, St. Gregory the Great asks: Who are these people who enter without the wedding garment? What is this garment and how does one acquire it? He replies that those who are invited and enter do in some way have faith. It is faith that opens the door to them. But they lack the wedding garment of love. Those who do not live their faith as love are not ready for the banquet and are cast out. Eucharistic communion requires faith, but faith requires love; otherwise, even as faith, it is dead. . . .

"I have earnestly desired to eat this Passover with you." Lord, you desire us, you desire me. You eagerly desire to share yourself with us in the Holy Eucharist, to be one with us. Lord, awaken in us the desire for you. Strengthen us in unity with you and with one another. Grant unity to your Church so that the world may believe. Amen.

—Homily, Holy Thursday, St. Peter's Basilica, April 21, 2011

Making a Sacrifice of Ourselves

The outpouring of Christ's blood is the source of the Church's life. St. John, as we know, sees in the water and blood that flowed from our Lord's body the wellspring of that divine life that is bestowed by the Holy Spirit and communicated to us in the sacraments (John 19:34; cf. 1 John 1:7; 5:6-7). The Letter to the Hebrews draws out, we might say, the liturgical implications of this mystery. Jesus, by his suffering and death, his self-oblation in the eternal Spirit, has become our high priest and "the mediator of a new covenant" (Hebrews 9:15). These words echo our Lord's own words at the Last Supper, when he instituted the Eucharist as the sacrament of his body, given up for us, and his blood, the blood of the new and everlasting covenant shed for the forgiveness of sins (cf. Mark 14:24, Matthew 26:28, Luke 22:20).

Faithful to Christ's command to "do this in remembrance of me" (Luke 22:19), the Church in every time and place celebrates the Eucharist until the Lord returns in glory, rejoicing in his sacramental presence and drawing upon the power of his saving sacrifice for the redemption of the world. The reality of the Eucharistic sacrifice has always been at the heart of Catholic faith. . . .

The Eucharistic sacrifice of the Body and Blood of Christ embraces, in turn, the mystery of our Lord's continuing passion in the members of his mystical body, the Church, in every age. The crucifix serves as a reminder that Christ, our eternal high priest, daily unites our own sacrifices, our own sufferings, our own needs, hopes, and aspirations, to the infinite merits of his sacrifice. Through him, with him, and in him, we lift up our own bodies as a sacrifice "holy and acceptable to God" (Romans 12:1). In this sense we are caught up in his eternal oblation, completing, as St. Paul says, in our flesh "what is lacking in Christ's afflictions for the sake of his body, . . . the Church" (Colossians 1:24). In the life of the Church, in her trials and tribulations, Christ continues, in the stark phrase of Pascal, "to be in agony until the end of the world" (*Pensées,* ed. Léon Brunschvicg [Paris: Hachette, 1905], 553).

—Homily, City of Westminster, September 18, 2010

Heaven Comes Down to Earth

St. John Mary Vianney liked to tell his parishioners, "Come to Communion. . . . It is true that you are not worthy of it, but you need it." With the knowledge of being inadequate because of sin but needful of nourishing ourselves with the love that the Lord offers us in the Eucharistic sacrament, let us renew our faith in the Real Presence of Christ in the Eucharist. We must not take this faith for granted! Today we run the risk of secularization creeping into the Church too. It can be translated into formal and empty Eucharistic worship, into celebrations lacking that heartfelt participation that is expressed in veneration and in respect for the liturgy. The temptation to reduce prayer to superficial, hasty moments, letting ourselves be overpowered by earthly activities and concerns, is always strong.

When, in a little while, we recite the Our Father, the prayer par excellence, we will say, "Give us this day our daily bread," thinking, of course, of the bread of each day for us and for all peoples. But this request contains something deeper. The Greek word *epioúsios* that we translate as "daily" could also allude to the "super-stantial" bread, the bread "of the world to come." Some Fathers of the Church saw this as a reference to the Eucharist, the bread of eternal life, the new world that is already given to us in Holy Mass, so that from this moment, the future world may begin within us. With the Eucharist, therefore, heaven comes down to earth, the future of God enters the present, and it is as though time were embraced by divine eternity.

. . . Stay with us, Jesus. Make a gift of yourself, and give us the bread that nourishes us for eternal life! Free this world from the poison of evil, violence, and hatred that pollute consciences, and purify it with the power of your merciful love. And you, Mary, who was the woman "of the Eucharist" throughout your life, help us to walk united toward the heavenly goal, nourished by the Body and Blood of Christ, the eternal Bread of life and medicine of divine immortality. Amen!

—Homily, Solemnity of Corpus Christi, Basilica of St. John Lateran,
June 11, 2009

MARY, WOMAN OF THE EUCHARIST

May Mary Most Holy, the Immaculate Virgin, ark of the new and eternal covenant, accompany us on our way to meet the Lord who comes. In her we find realized most perfectly the essence of the Church. The Church sees in Mary—"Woman of the Eucharist," as she was called by Pope John Paul II—her finest icon, and she contemplates Mary as a singular model of the Eucharistic life. . . . She is the *tota pulchra,* the all-beautiful, for in her the radiance of God's glory shines forth. The beauty of the heavenly liturgy, which must be reflected in our own assemblies, is faithfully mirrored in her. From Mary we must learn to become men and women of the Eucharist and of the Church, and thus to present ourselves, in the words of St. Paul, "holy and blameless" before the Lord, even as he wished us to be from the beginning (Colossians 1:22; Ephesians 1:4).

Through the intercession of the Blessed Virgin Mary, may the Holy Spirit kindle within us the same ardor experienced by the disciples on the way to Emmaus (cf. Luke 24:13-35) and renew our "Eucharistic wonder" through the splendor and beauty radiating from the liturgical rite, the efficacious sign of the infinite beauty of the holy mystery of God. Those disciples arose and returned in haste to Jerusalem in order to share their joy with their brothers and sisters in the faith. True joy is found in recognizing that the Lord is still with us, our faithful companion along the way. The Eucharist makes us discover that Christ, risen from the dead, is our contemporary in the mystery of the Church, his body. Of this mystery of love we have become witnesses. Let us encourage one another to walk joyfully, our hearts filled with wonder, toward our encounter with the Holy Eucharist so that we may experience and proclaim to others the truth of the words with which Jesus took leave of his disciples: "Lo, I am with you always, until the end of the world" (cf. Matthew 28:20).

—Apostolic Exhortation *Sacramentum Caritatis*, 96–97,
February 22, 2007

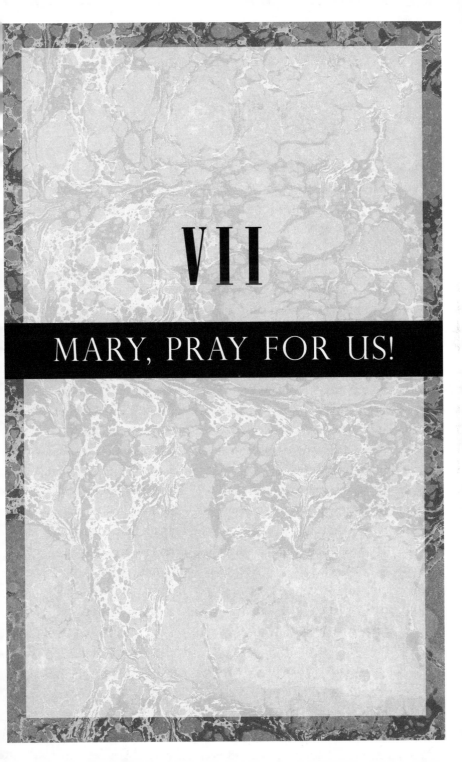

VII

MARY, PRAY FOR US!

Mary Speaks for Us All

What happened here in Nazareth, far from the gaze of the world, was a singular act of God, a powerful intervention in history, through which a child was conceived who was to bring salvation to the whole world. The wonder of the Incarnation continues to challenge us to open up our understanding to the limitless possibilities of God's transforming power, of his love for us, his desire to be united with us. Here the eternally begotten Son of God became man, and so made it possible for us, his brothers and sisters, to share in his divine sonship. That downward movement of self-emptying love made possible the upward movement of exaltation in which we, too, are raised to share in the life of God himself (cf. Philippians 2:6-11).

The Spirit who "came upon Mary" (cf. Luke 1:35) is the same Spirit who hovered over the waters at the dawn of creation (cf. Genesis 1:2). We are reminded that the Incarnation was a new creative act. When our Lord Jesus Christ was conceived in Mary's virginal womb through the power of the Holy Spirit, God united himself with our created humanity, entering into a permanent new relationship with us and ushering in a new creation. The narrative of the Annunciation illustrates God's extraordinary courtesy (cf. Julian of Norwich, *Revelations*, 77–79). He does not impose himself; he does not simply predetermine the part that Mary will play in his plan for our salvation; he first seeks her consent.

In the original creation, there was clearly no question of God seeking the consent of his creatures, but in this new creation he does so. Mary stands in the place of all humanity. She speaks for us all when she responds to the angel's invitation. St. Bernard describes how the whole court of heaven was waiting with eager anticipation for her word of consent that consummated the nuptial union between God and humanity. The attention of all the choirs of angels was riveted on this spot, where a dialogue took place that would launch a new and definitive chapter in world history. Mary said, "Let it be done to me according to your word" (cf. Luke 1:38). And the Word of God became flesh.

When we reflect on this joyful mystery, it gives us hope, the sure hope that God will continue to reach into our history, to act with creative power, so as to achieve goals which by human reckoning seem impossible. It challenges us to open ourselves to the transforming action of the Creator Spirit who makes us new, makes us one with him, and fills us with his life. It invites us, with exquisite courtesy, to consent to his dwelling within us, to welcome the Word of God into our hearts, enabling us to respond to him in love and to reach out in love toward one another.

—Homily, Nazareth, May 14, 2009

MARY, FULL OF GRACE, GIVE US CHRIST!

O Mary, Immaculate Virgin, . . . we greet you and call upon you with the angel's words: "full of grace" (Luke 1:28), the most beautiful name that God himself has called you from eternity.

"Full of grace" are you, Mary, full of divine love from the very first moment of your existence, providentially predestined to be Mother of the Redeemer and intimately connected to him in the mystery of salvation.

In your Immaculate Conception shines forth the vocation of Christ's disciples, called to become, with his grace, saints and immaculate through love (cf. Ephesians 1:5). In you shines the dignity of every human being who is always precious in the Creator's eyes.

Those who look to you, All Holy Mother, never lose their serenity, no matter what the hardships of life.

Although the experience of sin is a sad one since it disfigures the dignity of God's children, anyone who turns to you discovers the beauty of truth and love and finds the path that leads to the Father's house.

"Full of grace" are you, Mary, who with your "yes" to the Creator's plan opened to us the path of salvation. Teach us also at your school to say our "yes" to the Lord's will. Let it be a "yes" that joins with your own "yes" without reservations or shadows, a "yes" that the heavenly Father willed to have need of in order to beget the new man, Christ, the one Savior of the world and of history.

Give us the courage to say "no" to the deceptions of power, money, pleasure; to dishonest earnings, corruption, and hypocrisy; to selfishness and violence; "no" to the evil one, the deceitful prince of this world; to say "yes" to Christ, who destroys the power of evil with the omnipotence of love. We know that only hearts converted to love, which is God, can build a better future for all.

"Full of grace" are you, Mary! For all generations your name is a pledge of sure hope. Yes! Because as the great poet Dante wrote, for us mortals, you are "a source of living hope" (*Paradiso,* XXXIII, 12). Let us come once again as trusting pilgrims to draw faith and comfort, joy and love, safety and peace from this source, the wellspring of your Immaculate Heart.

Virgin *"full of grace,"* . . . show yourself as a provident and merciful Mother to the whole world so that by respecting human dignity and rejecting every form of violence and exploitation, sound foundations may be laid for the civilization of love.

Show yourself as Mother, especially to those most in need: the defenseless, the marginalized and outcasts, the victims of a society that all too often sacrifices the human person for other ends and interests.

Show yourself, O Mary, as Mother of all, and give us Christ, the hope of the world! *"Monstra Te esse Matrem,"* O Virgin Immaculate, full of grace! Amen!

—Prayer to Mary Immaculate, December 8, 2006

May We, Like Mary, Welcome God's Word

The Incarnation of the Son of God is the central mystery of the Christian faith, and in it Mary occupies a central place. But, we ask, what is the meaning of this mystery? And what importance does it have for our concrete lives?

First of all, let us see what the Incarnation means. In the Gospel of St. Luke, we heard the words of the angel to Mary: "The Holy Spirit will come upon you, / and the power of the Most High will overshadow you; / therefore the child to be born will be called holy, / the Son of God" (Luke 1:35). In Mary, the Son of God is made man, fulfilling in this way the prophecy of Isaiah: "Behold, a young woman shall conceive and bear a son, and shall call his name Immanuel, which means 'God-with-us'" (Isaiah 7:14). Jesus, the Word made flesh, is truly God-with-us, who has come to live among us and to share our human condition.

The apostle St. John expresses it in the following way: "And the Word became flesh and dwelt among us" (John 1:14). The expression "became flesh" points to our human reality in a most concrete and tangible way. In Christ, God has truly come into the world; he has entered into our history; he has set his dwelling among us, thus fulfilling the deepest desire of human beings, that the world may truly become a home worthy of humanity. On the other hand, when God is put aside, the world becomes an inhospitable place for man and frustrates creation's true vocation to be a space for the covenant, for the "yes" to the love between

God and humanity who responds to him. Mary did so as the first fruit of believers with her unreserved "yes" to the Lord.

For this reason, contemplating the mystery of the Incarnation, we cannot fail to turn our eyes to her so as to be filled with wonder, gratitude, and love at seeing how our God, coming into the world, wished to depend upon the free consent of one of his creatures. Only from the moment when the Virgin responded to the angel, "Behold, I am the handmaid of the Lord; let it be to me according to your word" (Luke 1:38), did the eternal Word of the Father begin his human existence in time. It is touching to see how God not only respects human freedom; he almost seems to require it. And we see also how the beginning of the earthly life of the Son of God was marked by a double "yes" to the saving plan of the Father—that of Christ and that of Mary. This obedience to God is what opens the doors of the world to the truth, to salvation. God has created us as the fruit of his infinite love; hence, to live in accordance with his will is the way to encounter our genuine identity, the truth of our being, while apart from God, we are alienated from ourselves and are hurled into the void. The obedience of faith is true liberty, authentic redemption, which allows us to unite ourselves to the love of Jesus in his determination to conform himself to the will of the Father. Redemption is always this process of the lifting up of the human will to full communion with the divine will.

Dear brothers and sisters, today we praise the Most Holy Virgin for her faith, and with St. Elizabeth we, too, say, "Blessed is she who believed" (Luke 1:45). As St. Augustine said, Mary conceived Christ by faith in her heart before she conceived him physically in her womb; Mary believed, and what she believed came to be in her (cf. *Sermo* 215, 4: PL 38, 1074). Let us ask the Lord to strengthen our faith, to make it active and fruitful in love. Let us implore him that, like her, we may welcome the word of God into our hearts and carry it out with docility and constancy.

—Homily, Solemnity of the Annunciation of the Lord, Cuba,
March 26, 2012

The Word of God and Marian Prayer

Mindful of the inseparable bond between the word of God and Mary of Nazareth, along with the Synod Fathers, I urge that Marian prayer be encouraged among the faithful, above all in the life of families, since it is an aid to meditating on the holy mysteries found in the Scriptures. A most helpful aid, for example, is the individual or communal recitation of the Holy Rosary, which ponders the mysteries of Christ's life in union with Mary and which Pope John Paul II wished to enrich with the mysteries of light. It is fitting that the announcement of each mystery be accompanied by a brief biblical text pertinent to that mystery, so as to encourage the memorization of brief biblical passages relevant to the mysteries of Christ's life.

The Synod also recommended that the faithful be encouraged to pray the Angelus. This prayer, simple yet profound, allows us "to commemorate daily the mystery of the Incarnate Word"

(*Propositio*, 55). It is only right that the People of God, families and communities of consecrated persons, be faithful to this Marian prayer, traditionally recited at sunrise, midday, and sunset. In the Angelus we ask God to grant that, through Mary's intercession, we may imitate her in doing his will and in welcoming his word into our lives. This practice can help us to grow in an authentic love for the mystery of the Incarnation.

The ancient prayers of the Christian East that contemplate the entire history of salvation in the light of the *Theotokos*, the Mother of God, are likewise worthy of being known, appreciated, and widely used. Here particular mention can be made of the *Akathist* and *Paraklesis* prayers. These hymns of praise, chanted in the form of a litany and steeped in the faith of the Church and in references to the Bible, help the faithful to meditate on the mysteries of Christ in union with Mary. In particular, the venerable *Akathist* hymn to the Mother of God—so-called because it is sung while standing—represents one of the highest expressions of the Marian piety of the Byzantine tradition. Praying with these words opens wide the heart and disposes it to the peace that is from above, from God, to that peace which is Christ himself, born of Mary for our salvation.

—Apostolic Exhortation *Verbum Domini*, 88, September 30, 2010

Praising God with Mary's Spirit and Soul

[The Magnificat] is a canticle that reveals in filigree the spirituality of the biblical *anawim*, that is, of those faithful who, not only recognize themselves as "poor" in the detachment from all idolatry of riches and power, but also in the profound humility of a heart emptied of the temptation to pride and open to the bursting in of the divine saving grace. Indeed, the whole Magnificat is marked by this "humility," in Greek, *tapeinosis,* which indicates a situation of material humility and poverty.

The first part of the Marian canticle (cf. Luke 1:46-50) is a sort of solo voice that rises to heaven to reach the Lord. The constant resonance of the first person should be noted: "My soul . . . / my spirit . . . my Savior / . . . has done great things for me / . . . [They] will call me blessed. . . ." So it is that the soul of the prayer is the celebration of the divine grace that has burst into the heart and life of Mary, making her mother of the Lord. We hear the Virgin's own voice speaking of her Savior who has done great things in her soul and body.

The intimate structure of her prayerful canticle, therefore, is praise, thanksgiving, and grateful joy. But this personal witness is neither solitary nor . . . purely individualistic, because the Virgin Mother is aware that she has a mission to fulfill for humanity, and her experience fits into the history of salvation.

She can thus say, "And his mercy is on those who fear him / from generation to generation" (Luke 1:50). With this praise of the Lord, Our Lady gives a voice to all redeemed creatures, who find in her *fiat*, and thus in the figure of Jesus born of the Virgin, the mercy of God.

It is at this point that the second poetic and spiritual part of the Magnificat unfolds (cf. Luke 1:51-55). It has a more choral tone, almost as if the voices of the whole community of the faithful were associated with Mary's voice, celebrating God's amazing decision.

In the original Greek of Luke's Gospel, we have seven aorist verbs that indicate the same number of actions that the Lord carries out repeatedly in history: "He has shown strength / . . . he has scattered the proud / . . . he has put down the mighty / . . . he has exalted those of low degree / . . . he has filled the hungry with good things / . . . the rich he has sent empty away / . . . he has helped . . . Israel."

In these seven divine acts, the "style" that inspires the behavior of the Lord of history stands out: he takes the part of the lowly. His plan is one that is often hidden beneath the opaque context of human events that see "the proud, the mighty, and the rich" triumph.

Yet his secret strength is destined in the end to be revealed, to show who God's true favorites are: "those who fear him," faithful to his words, "those of low degree," "the hungry," "his servant Israel"; in other words, the community of the People of God who, like Mary, consist of people who are "poor," pure, and simple of heart. It is that "little flock" that is told not to fear, for the Lord has been pleased to give it his kingdom (cf. Luke 12:32). And this canticle invites us to join the tiny flock and the true members of the People of God in purity and simplicity of heart, in God's love.

Let us therefore accept the invitation that St. Ambrose, the great Doctor of the Church, addresses to us in his commentary on the text of the Magnificat:

> May Mary's soul be in each one to magnify the Lord, may Mary's spirit be in each one to rejoice in God; if, according to the flesh, the Mother of Christ is one alone, according to the faith all souls bring forth Christ; each, in fact, welcomes the Word of God within. . . . Mary's soul magnifies the Lord and her spirit rejoices in God because, consecrated in soul and spirit to the Father and to the Son, she adores with devout affection one God, from whom come all things and only one Lord, by virtue of whom all things exist. (*Exposition of the Holy Gospel according to Saint Luke 2:26-27*, collected in *SAEMO*, XI [Milan-Rome: Bibliotheca Ambrosiana Citta Nuova Editrice, 1978], 169)

In this marvelous commentary on the Magnificat by St. Ambrose, I am always especially moved by the surprising words: "If, according to the flesh, the Mother of Christ is one alone, according to the faith all souls bring forth Christ"—indeed, each one intimately welcomes the Word of God. Thus, interpreting Our Lady's very words, the holy Doctor invites us to ensure that the Lord can find a dwelling place in our own souls and lives. Not only must we carry him in our hearts, but we must bring him to the world so that we, too, can bring forth Christ for our epoch. Let us pray to the Lord to help us praise him with Mary's spirit and soul, and to bring Christ back to our world.

—General Audience, Paul VI Audience Hall, February 15, 2006

MARY, SPEAK TO US OF JESUS

Mary, Mother of the "Yes," you listened to Jesus,
and know the tone of his voice and the beating of his heart.
Morning Star, speak to us of him,
and tell us about your journey of following him on the path
    of faith.

Mary, who dwelt with Jesus in Nazareth,
impress on our lives your sentiments,
your docility, your attentive silence,
and make the Word flourish in genuinely free choices.

Mary, speak to us of Jesus, so that the freshness of our faith
shines in our eyes and warms the heart of those we meet,
as you did when visiting Elizabeth,
who in her old age rejoiced with you for the gift of life.

Mary, Virgin of the Magnificat,
help us to bring joy to the world and, as at Cana,
lead every young person involved in service of others
to do only what Jesus will tell them. . . .

Mary, Our Lady of Loreto, Gate of Heaven,
help us to lift our eyes on high.
We want to see Jesus, to speak with him,
to proclaim his love to all.

—Prayer at the Shrine of Loreto and Holy House,
September 1, 2007

CONTEMPLATING MARY IN HEAVENLY GLORY

Since the first centuries of Christianity, the Christian people has always found this feast [of the Assumption] deeply stirring; as is well-known, it celebrates the glorification, also in body, of that creature whom God chose as mother and whom Jesus on the cross gave as mother to the whole of humanity.

The Assumption evokes a mystery that concerns each one of us because, as the Second Vatican Council affirms, Mary "shines forth on earth, . . . a sign of sure hope and solace to the People of God during its sojourn on earth" (*Lumen Gentium,* 68).

However, taken up by the events of each day, one can sometimes forget this comforting spiritual reality that constitutes an important truth of faith; so how can it be ensured that this luminous sign of hope is ever more clearly perceived by all of us and by contemporary society?

Some people today live as if they never had to die, or as if, with death, everything were over; others, who hold that man is the one and only author of his own destiny, behave as though God did not exist, and at times they even reach the point of denying that there is room for him in our world.

Yet the great breakthroughs of technology and science that have considerably improved humanity's condition leave unresolved the deepest searchings of the human soul.

Only openness to the mystery of God, who is Love, can quench the thirst for truth and happiness in our hearts; only the prospect of eternity can give authentic value to historical events and especially to the mystery of human frailty, suffering, and death.

By contemplating Mary in heavenly glory, we understand that the earth is not the definitive homeland for us either and that, if we live with our gaze fixed on eternal goods, we will one day share in this same glory, and the earth will become more beautiful.

Consequently, we must not lose our serenity and peace even amid the thousands of daily difficulties. The luminous sign of Our Lady taken up into heaven shines out even more brightly when sad shadows of suffering and violence seem to loom on the horizon.

We may be sure of it: from on high Mary follows our footsteps with gentle concern, dispels the gloom in moments of darkness and distress, and reassures us with her motherly hand.

Supported by this awareness, let us continue confidently on our path of Christian commitment wherever Providence may lead us. Let us forge ahead in our lives under Mary's guidance.

—General Audience, Castel Gandolfo, August 16, 2006

MARY, STAR OF THE SEA,
TEACH US TO HOPE

With a hymn composed in the eighth or ninth century, thus for over a thousand years, the Church has greeted Mary, the Mother of God, as "Star of the Sea": *Ave maris stella.* Human life is a journey. Toward what destination? How do we find the way? Life is like a voyage on the sea of history, often dark and stormy, a voyage in which we watch for the stars that indicate the route. The true stars of our life are the people who have lived good lives. They are lights of hope. Certainly, Jesus Christ is the true light, the sun that has risen above all the shadows of history.

But to reach him, we also need lights close by—people who shine with his light and so guide us along our way. Who more than Mary could be a star of hope for us? With her "yes" she opened the door of our world to God himself; she became the living Ark of the Covenant, in whom God took flesh, became one of us, and pitched his tent among us (cf. John 1:14).

So we cry to her: Holy Mary, you belonged to the humble and great souls of Israel who, like Simeon, were "looking for the consolation of Israel" (Luke 2:25) and hoping, like Anna, "for the redemption of Jerusalem" (2:38). Your life was thoroughly imbued with the Sacred Scriptures of Israel, which spoke of hope, of the promise made to Abraham and his descendants (cf. 1:55). In this way we can appreciate the holy fear that overcame you when the angel of the Lord appeared to you and told you that you would give birth to the One who was the hope of Israel, the One awaited by the world.

Through you, through your "yes," the hope of the ages became reality, entering this world and its history. You bowed low before the greatness of this task and gave your consent: "Behold, I am the handmaid of the Lord; let it be to me according to your word" (Luke 1:38). When you hastened with holy joy across the mountains of Judea to see your cousin Elizabeth, you became the image of the Church to come, which carries the hope of the world in her womb across the mountains of history. But alongside the joy which, with your Magnificat, you proclaimed in word and song for all the centuries to hear, you also knew the dark sayings of the prophets about the suffering of the servant of God in this world. Shining over his birth in the stable at Bethlehem, there were angels in splendor who brought the good news to the shepherds, but at the same time, the lowliness of God in this world was all too palpable. The old man Simeon spoke to you of the sword which would pierce your soul (cf. 2:35), of the sign of contradiction that your Son would be in this world.

Then, when Jesus began his public ministry, you had to step aside so that a new family could grow, the family that it was his mission to establish and that would be made up of those who heard his word and kept it (cf. Luke 11:27-28). Notwithstanding the great joy that marked the beginning of Jesus' ministry, in the synagogue of Nazareth, you must already have experienced the truth of the saying about the "sign of contradiction" (cf. 4:28ff.).

In this way you saw the growing power of hostility and rejection that built up around Jesus until the hour of the cross, when you had to look upon the Savior of the world, the heir of David, the Son of God dying like a failure, exposed to mockery, between criminals. Then you received the word of Jesus: "Woman, behold, your Son!" (John 19:26). From the cross you received a new mission. From the cross you became a mother in a new way: the mother of all those who believe in your Son Jesus and wish to follow him. The sword of sorrow pierced your heart. Did hope die? Did the world remain definitively without light, and life without purpose?

At that moment, deep down, you probably listened again to the word spoken by the angel in answer to your fear at the time of the Annunciation: "Do not be afraid, Mary!" (Luke 1:30). How many times had the Lord, your Son, said the same thing to his disciples: Do not be afraid! In your heart you heard this word again during the night of Golgotha. Before the hour of his betrayal, he had said to his disciples, "Be of good cheer, I have overcome the world" (John 16:33). "Let not your hearts be troubled, neither let them be afraid" (14:27). "Do not be afraid, Mary!" In that hour at Nazareth, the angel had also said to you: "Of his kingdom there will be no end" (Luke 1:30, 33). Could it have ended before it began? No, at the foot of the cross, on the strength of Jesus' own word, you became the mother of believers. In this faith, which even in the darkness of Holy Saturday bore the certitude of hope, you made your way toward Easter morning.

The joy of the resurrection touched your heart and united you in a new way to the disciples, destined to become the family of Jesus through faith. In this way you were in the midst of the community of believers, who in the days following the Ascension prayed with one voice for the gift of the Holy

Spirit (cf. Acts 1:14) and then received that gift on the day of Pentecost. The "kingdom" of Jesus was not as might have been imagined. It began in that hour, and of this "kingdom" there will be no end. Thus, you remain in the midst of the disciples as their Mother, as the Mother of Hope. Holy Mary, Mother of God, our Mother, teach us to believe, to hope, to love with you. Show us the way to his kingdom! Star of the Sea, shine upon us and guide us on our way!

—Encyclical *Spe Salvi*, 49–50, November 30, 2007

A PRAYER TO THE MOTHER OF MERCY

Obedient Virgin, Mother of Christ, who with your docile "yes" to the angel's announcement became the Mother of the Almighty, help all your children to follow the plans that the heavenly Father has for each one, in order to cooperate in the universal plan of redemption that Christ fulfilled by dying on the cross.

Virgin of Nazareth, Queen of the family, make our Christian families schools of evangelical life, enriched by the gift of many vocations to the priesthood and to the consecrated life. Keep intact the unity of our families, today so threatened from all sides, making them hearths of serenity and of harmony, where patient dialogue dispels difficulties and differences. Above all, watch over those who are divided and in crisis, Mother of forgiveness and reconciliation. . . .

Clement Virgin, Mother of humanity, turn your gaze to the men and women of our time, to peoples and to those who govern them, to nations and to continents. Comfort those who weep, who suffer, who struggle because of human injustice. Sustain those who waver under the weight of effort and who look at the future without hope. Encourage those who work to build a better world where justice triumphs and brotherhood reigns, where selfishness, hate, and violence cease. May every form and manifestation of violence be conquered by the peacemaking power of Christ.

Virgin of listening, Star of Hope, Mother of Mercy, the source through which Jesus came into the world, our life and our joy, we thank you and we renew the offering of our lives, certain that you will never abandon us, especially in the dark and difficult moments of life. Be with us always, now and at the hour of our death. Amen!

—Prayer to Our Lady, September 6, 2009

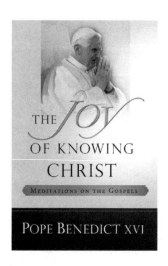

The Joy of Knowing Christ
Meditations on the Gospels

"The passages in this book guide us on a journey through the life of Christ. They begin with meditations on Mary, encompass Jesus' suffering and resurrection, and reach their climax at Pentecost. Every step of the way, Pope Benedict invites us to open ourselves to the truth. Through his words, God reaches out to us in passionate love and unending mercy, knowing exactly who we are and what we need."

—**Amy Welborn**, author of *Come Meet Jesus: An Invitation from Pope Benedict XVI*

5¼ x 8, softcover, 144 pages, $11.95
Item# BPBDE9

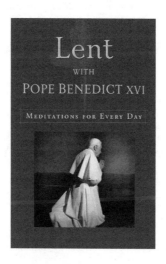

Lent with Pope Benedict XVI
Meditations for Every Day

"Lent with Pope Benedict XVI is an opportunity to experience our Holy Father once again as a sensitive spiritual director and a teacher of profound wisdom. As he guides us through each day of Lent, he shows us that Christ is our 'sturdy support' and the source of that 'indispensable spiritual energy' we need to live in peace and happiness. The meditations in this book will nurture you on your Lenten journey so that at Easter, you can experience all over again the joy of the risen Lord and the new life he came to bring us."
—Cardinal Donald Wuerl,
Archbishop of Washington

5¼ x 8, softcover, 144 pages, $11.95
Item# BPBFE2

the WORD among us ®

The *Spirit* of Catholic Living

This book was published by The Word Among Us. Since 1981, The Word Among Us has been answering the call of the Second Vatican Council to help Catholic laypeople encounter Christ in the Scriptures.

The name of our company comes from the prologue to the Gospel of John and reflects the vision and purpose of all of our publications: to be an instrument of the Spirit, whose desire is to manifest Jesus' presence in and to the children of God. In this way, we hope to contribute to the Church's ongoing mission of proclaiming the gospel to the world so that all people would know the love and mercy of our Lord and grow ever more deeply in love with him.

Our monthly devotional magazine, *The Word Among Us*, features meditations on the daily and Sunday Mass readings, and currently reaches more than one million Catholics in North America and another half million Catholics in one hundred countries around the world. Our book division, The Word Among Us Press, publishes numerous books, Bible studies, and pamphlets that help Catholics grow in their faith.

To learn more about who we are and what we publish, log on to our website at www.wau.org. There you will find a variety of Catholic resources that will help you grow in your faith.

Embrace His Word, Listen to God . . .